ANDRE DUBUS

A Study of the Short Fiction

Twayne's Studies in Short Fiction

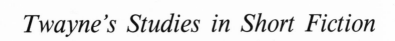

Gordon Weaver, General Editor
Oklahoma State University

Andre Dubus.
*Illustration reprinted by permission of the artist, Lewis Thompson,
and the* Hollins Critic.

ANDRE DUBUS

A Study of the Short Fiction

Thomas E. Kennedy

TWAYNE PUBLISHERS • BOSTON
A Division of G. K. Hall & Co.

Twayne's Studies in Short Fiction Series No. 1
Editorial Assistant to Gordon Weaver: Stephanie Corcoran

Published by Twayne Publishers
A Division of G. K. Hall & Co.
70 Lincoln Street, Boston, Massachusetts 02111

Copyedition supervised by Barbara Sutton.
Book design by Janet Zietowski.
Book production by Gabrielle B. McDonald.
Typeset in 10/12 Times Roman by Williams Press, Inc.

Printed on permanent/durable acid-free paper
and bound in the United States of America.

Library of Congress Cataloging-in-Publication Data

Kennedy, Thomas E., 1944–
    Andre Dubus: a study of the short fiction / Thomas E. Kennedy.
      p. cm.—(Twayne's studies in short ficiton: TSSF 1)
    Bibliography: p.
    Includes index.
    ISBN 0-8057-8305-9 (alk. paper)
    1. Dubus, Andre, 1936– —Criticism and interpretation.
I Title. II. Series.
PS3554.U265Z74 1988
813'.54—dc19
                                        88-10976
                                          CIP

Contents

Preface*

"There are no events but words in fiction," William H. Gass wrote in *Fiction and the Figures of Life* (1971). "How absurd these views are which think of fiction as . . . actually creative of living creatures." He also observed: "That novels should be made of words, and merely words, is shocking, really. It's as though you had discovered that your wife were made of rubber."

The argument is useful as a theoretical instrument with which to measure the dimensions of postmodern literature. Some writers—Gass, John Barth, Stanley Elkins, Robert Coover, Donald Barthelme, Gordon Weaver, Gladys Swan, to name a few—seem to turn from fictional sociology to explore language, perception, imagination, the craft of fiction itself, in a search to identify a deeper existential reality.

Andre Dubus is *not* such a writer.

At a time when, for better or worse, American fiction has shown a certain tendency to focus upon the navel of its own technique and many writers have abandoned the attempt to deal directly with reality, the fiction of Andre Dubus has distinguished itself as indefatigably realistic, consistently concerned with an existential Christian vision of a real world in which real human beings must live, a temporal span which, being alive, they must traverse and within which, faced daily by choice, they must act and take responsibility for the consequences of those actions.

Dubus was a young journeyman at Iowa when the postmodern wave began to swell along the surface of American fiction; it passed Dubus without mussing his hair. As John Updike has said of him, Dubus beat the neorealists to it by twenty years. His characters are people, imagined lives whose blood and flesh are sketched in words, experiencing events in a mirror of the world.

Dubus began to publish in the 1960s, a decade whose fictional spearhead in America declared war on realism. Overloaded perhaps

* A portion of this preface originally appeared in the *Sewanee Review* 95, no. 2 (1987):39–41, and in *Delta* 24 (1987):91–101.

with the sociopolitical gore being spewed out daily from news-papers, television screens, and radios concerning foreign war and domestic strife, many American fiction writers began to retreat to more purely imaginative realms, to an overt contemplation of the technical implements of their craft: Latin American magical realism, the Barthelme jump-cut collage, the Cooverian infinite replay with variations, the Hawkes time shuffle, the Burroughs page shuffle, the Barthian anti-illusionist illusion. It was a decade whose best-selling novels depicted American society as a madhouse run by a madwoman or snagged on a catch clause, whose heroes were a wild nihilistic Gingerman, an epic onanist, a computer-assisted goatboy; a decade when novels took the form of psychiatric rants climaxing in lengthy Janovian primal screams, of cold-blooded facts fleshed into bloody fiction that followed real-life killers to the gallows, of subjectivized journalism parading as instant historical novel; when even an established sometime-realist like Malamud was publishing stories with birds whose vocabulary made Poe's raven look dumb and novels whose protagonist de-bated with the devil over the artistic form and content of a hole in the ground, a grave.

A "new" fiction was proclaimed by theorists like Joe David Bellamy, which in retrospect seems less new than reactionary, in a nonpejorative sense of the word—a rejection of the form that had evolved in the immediate past century to hark back to techniques closer to those of subjective-romantics such as Haw-thorne and Poe or to the absurdist strategies of Gogol or the earlier experiments of Sterne. The story of manners—developed to fine subtleties and nuances by Flaubert, Chekhov, and James, who used the intricacies of human behavior as metaphor for the drift of movement of the spirit, making their abstractions from the mystery in which human beings daily live—was largely rejected as insufficient to deal with the immediate political pressures seen to be stifling the spirit of humanism. And people just plain wanted something new. *Innovation* was the word of the hour. Hallowed, ivied institutions were awarding honorary doctoral degrees to a young, wandering, college-dropout minstrel who sang, "Come writ-ers and critics who prophesy with your pen. . . . The times they are a-changing."

In this environment, ex–Marine Corps Captain Andre Dubus, pursuing a master of fine arts degree in the heart of the heart of

American university writing programs, was working out an arrestingly original story dramatizing a line in St. John, in which Christ prays to the Father, "I do not ask that You keep them out of the world, but that You keep them from evil."

The story, "If They Knew Yvonne," published in the *North American Review* in 1969, selected by Martha Foley as one of the *Best American Short Stories* of that year, and later collected in *Separate Flights* (Boston: Godine, 1975), might in many ways be viewed as a key and keynote for the nine books of fiction to follow from Dubus over the next two decades.

Dubus leaves the process of solving his technical writing problems on his desk; the only problems addressed by his stories are directly human, moral ones. The world of Dubus's fiction is one in which the word *sin* again becomes valid, for it is a world in which men and women are responsible for their actions, capable of wrong and perhaps also, therefore, of *right,* capable at least of seeking to avoid evil, at the very least of regretting the evil for which they are responsible, and in their commitment to this, of approaching love, communion with the God who issued the new command: to love one another.

This "rediscovery" of sin and, perhaps more important, the identification of sin as an affront against the human beings for whom we are responsible, to whom we must commit ourselves if we are to "tap our souls on the march to death" ("Going Under," *SF*), is, I believe, a vital part of Dubus's fiction: How have we not lived right? In what way are we adulterating ourselves and the love that is essential to life? What are the consequences of our acts when we know not what we do?

I do not mean to imply that a visit to Dubus's world is like entering a revival tent. On the contrary, these fictions occur in a world of moral complexity. We meet few black-and-whites here. We witness human beings turning on the spit of their humanity. But we also witness moments of moral epiphany, recognitions for the character, or at least for the reader, that give sometimes the liberation, sometimes the burden of comprehension and self-awareness—or sometimes simply the enigma at the heart of our desire to live well, to grow well.

The vision of the world Dubus draws is certain of its values, rejects cynicism and self-contempt and depression with swift, deft movements toward the opposites of these moral disabilities—but, again, with no moral simplifications: The father who covers up his daughter's hit-and-run crime in "A Father's Story" must admit to himself, "I love her more than I love truth," and it is a hard moment for him, one whose consequences touch the remainder of his life.

Love is as natural an element here as air or water and is treated in a direct, unashamed way, devoid of cynicism or dark laughter. Without it, the spirit shrivels, demons of madness are unleashed, priests lose contact with their faith, mothers and fathers lose contact with one another and themselves and their children. With it, Dubus's characters know pain, but also come to understand both the distance from and closeness to the beloved and to experience sacramental moments of communion. Yet even love, even a love of pure motive, has consequences and effects that are ambiguous, that exact a price of the purity of an individual's heart.

Love in Dubus's world is necessary, but is also a high spiritual state which can be approached only when it has been distinguished from the solipsistic hungers of the lonely spirit, a process that requires self-awareness and an acceptance of responsibility for one's actions and for those one loves. One must know more than the pleasure of touch upon one's own body ("His Lover," *FGA*); one must know one's own heart.

These are the matters with which Dubus deals in his fiction, tracing the everyday tragedies of ordinary Americans today to the moral blindness, isolation, and severed social, familial, and behavioral roots from which they develop. Dubus's subjects and themes make an interesting contrast with those of much of the prominent fiction of the sixties, seventies, and eighties. The content is not always dissimilar to Dubus's, but the approach and effect often are vastly different.

Perhaps it is Dubus's unashamed humanism that most distinguishes his work among that of his contemporaries. Frederick Busch has said, "The characters are bent beneath a weight that Andre Dubus, one feels, would bear for them if he could—their utterly plausible and undefined humanness, the terrible freight that children and parents carry to each other."

One of the great pleasures of reading Dubus's fiction is the relief of doffing the armor of cynicism and opening one's heart to the joys and pains of characters as near to living creatures as fictional creations can be, characters to whom we are introduced with equal measures of compassion and honesty.

About the Methodology

There is a group encounter experiment in which, on a given signal, each person in the group must move as quickly as possible to stand shoulder-to-shoulder with the one person he feels closest to in the group. The surprise of the experiment is that on the signal, everyone leaps into a movement that results in a single, tight sphere of human beings. It takes a moment to understand what has happened: the expectation is that individuals seeking individuals will cause fragmentation. But the result is unity; all are drawn together, and it is not possible to distinguish who has sought whom, who has been singled out; the entire group coheres in the sum total of each individual's desire to love another individual.

I mention this not so much as a thematic tie-in to the short fiction of Andre Dubus—although there is a thematic relationship: in the singling out of one human being by another in the process of human love, the human race coheres and continues itself, and this is an important part of the thematic background of Dubus's work. Rather, I refer to the exercise to dramatize the methodological problem of grouping Dubus's stories. They do lend themselves to six rather distinct subject groups. But as the kindred stories are placed shoulder to shoulder, the groups themselves begin to intermingle thematically until finally, rather than discovering a process of differentiation, one has confirmed the unity of the writer's artistic concerns.

Nonetheless, the half a hundred short and long stories Dubus has published so far do tend to fall into half a dozen subject categories: the Paul Clement stories and other tales of childhood, the stories about women and girls, the stories of military life, the stories about violence, those about love, and those about fatherhood. Interestingly, each of the categories contains roughly the same number of stories. Of course, there is a certain amount of overlap between these groupings. "Rose," for example, is primarily a long story about a woman, but it is also about violence, a failing marriage, a father disjointed from his role, a mother disjointed from hers, and it involves significant thematic similarities with some of the stories of military life and at least one of the Paul Clement stories. Looking at the *thematic* concerns of the stories, we find even greater overlap between the groupings, but I do not see this as a methodological problem for this study so much as an indication of Dubus's consistency of vision as a writer of fiction. As different as the subjects and surfaces may be, again and again, when we consider the elements of the stories, working in toward their cores, we find the same or similar or related elements of the basic structure of that vision: moral blindness, isolation, the lack of self-knowledge, the confusion between hunger and love.

Therefore, for the purposes of this study, I have chosen to consider the stories by their subject groupings—although I have not hesitated to employ ample thematic cross-references between the subject groupings—rather than to take them up either chronologically or according to the volume in which they were collected. Those readers wishing to make a systematic collection-by-collection study will be able to do so by use of the index.

I believe that this method will best facilitate the organization of a coherent critical overview of the short fiction of Andre Dubus.

About Text References

All page references will be to the texts published by David R. Godine, as follows, with the volume title abbreviations as indicated in parentheses: *Separate Flights (SF)* 1975; *Adultery & Other Choices (AOC)*, 1977; *Finding a Girl in America (FGA)*, 1980; *The Times Are Never So Bad (TNSB)*, 1983; *Voices from the Moon (VFM)*, 1984; *The Last Worthless Evening (LWE)*, 1986. Except where otherwise indicated, the Dubus quotes at the beginning of each chapter in part 1 are from the notes I collected interviewing him.

I owe an enormous debt of gratitude to Andre Dubus and Gordon Weaver, both of whom have given so generously of that scarcest of a writer's commodities: time. Andre Dubus spent many, many hours speaking into a tape recorder to answer the multitude of questions I typed up and sent across the Atlantic Ocean to him at a point when I did not yet know that I would write this book. Gordon Weaver's tireless willingness to read and reread manuscripts and to offer advice informed by his expert eye as fiction writer, editor, and professor has been indispensable. I would also like to express my appreciation to the editors of journals who published my first studies of the work of Andre Dubus— Patrick Samway and Claude Richard of *Delta;* George Core of the *Sewanee Review;* and John Rees Moore of the *Hollins Critic.*

Finally, I would like to dedicate this work with love to my dear wife and children: Monique, Daniel, Isabel.

Thomas E. Kennedy

Copenhagen, Denmark

THE SHORT FICTION:
A CRITICAL ANALYSIS

Childhood:
The Paul Clement Stories and
Other Tales of Youth

I have six children. I remember my childhood. I think
children know a lot, and I think a child certainly can
understand . . . that he himself bears some responsibility.

—Andre Dubus

The fiction of Andre Dubus is realistic, humanistic, and spiritual.
By the instrument of verisimilitude, he mirrors life. He is concerned with human beings, views his characters as real persons
experiencing real events in a real world. He is concerned about
what they do and takes their responsibility for their actions seriously.

Even the children in Dubus's fiction have or win some awareness
of their moral predicaments, a fact that brings to mind John
Barth's ironic observation in the title story of *Lost in the Funhouse*
that, whether real or valid, the dictates of sound fictional verisimilitude preclude certain psychological complexities in the fictional representation of children. Although not a technical innovator, Dubus is untroubled by any such facet of verisimilitude:
the children of his stories experience a moral existence no less
complex than the adults. Of the five Paul Clement stories to date,
three concern children in situations of moral and psychological
development, and one deals with a young man whose herd spirit
and sense of manhood drive him to sin against friendship. All
concern betrayal of one sort or another, life's earliest lessons
concerning the attempt to purchase survival at the expense of
connection.

In "If They Knew Yvonne" *(SF),* we meet a youngster so
concerned to preserve his faith *and* his sanity that he takes a
stand against the clerical negation of human sexuality and defines
for himself what sin is—a situation with interesting contrasts to

3

The Short Fiction: A Critical Analysis

Philip Roth's "The Conversion of the Jews; (in *Goodbye, Columbus*) and *Portnoy's Complaint.*

"The New Boy" *(TNSB)*, "Delivering" *(FGA)*, and the very short novel *Voices from the Moon* also deal with children whose humanity Dubus presents in an untraditionally fully developed state, and whose moral choices are as complex as those of adults. In "Delivering," a young teenaged boy overhears an argument between his mother and father and learns that his mother, helpless against her desire for another man, is leaving; the father weeps, but the boy reacts by steeling himself against sorrow and taking upon himself the task of toughening his younger brother. Young Walter of "The New Boy" is also a victim of divorce; here it is the father who leaves to live with a much younger woman. In the course of the story, Walter discovers that his mother and sisters, too, are sexual beings and avenges his loss of innocence by disposing of the diaphragms he finds in their rooms. In *Voices from the Moon,* Richie must also learn to live with his parents' divorce, and he does learn, although the process takes a piece of his heart. In "Dressed Like Summer Leaves" *(LWE)*, a boy is, in a sense, held responsible for his innocence, called to account for a lighthearted attitude toward war.

The Paul Clement stories are probably the most complex and evocative of the childhood tales, perhaps particularly because of the cumulative effect of focusing on the same character. Four of the five Paul Clement stories appear in Dubus's second collection, *Adultery & Other Choices (AOC)*: the first three of them consecutively—"An Afternoon with the Old Man," "Contrition," "The Bully"—and the fourth, "Cadence," following later in the volume. The fifth Paul Clement piece, "Goodbye," appears in a later collection, *The Times Are Never So Bad (TNSB)*.

The five stories are roughly chronological, the first three dealing with a boy, the fourth with a boy on the brink of manhood, the fifth with a young military officer going off with his wife, taking leave of his parents and of their unhappiness.

As fascinating as the moral complexities presented by some of the Paul Clement stories are, however, another of Dubus's youngsters, Harry Dugal, seems to offer a more comprehensive introduction to the writer's theme, and any discussion of Dubus's fiction would seem well advised to begin there. Published in the *North American Review* in 1969, selected by Martha Foley for the

4

Childhood: The Paul Clement Stories

1970 *Best American Short Stories* anthology, and reprinted in Dubus's first collection, *Separate Flights* (1975), "If They Knew Yvonne" keynotes the existential Christian vision at the core of Dubus's fiction.

The story follows the struggle of a young Roman Catholic, Harry Dugal, to find his way clear of the *via negativa,* which nearly destroys his relationship to his religion, and back into the world of human beings with his faith intact and functional. That journey finds its completion in a line from St. John, in which Christ prays to the Father, "I do not ask that You keep them out of the world, but that You keep them from evil."

This problem is central to the fiction of Dubus. How to live out one's part in a material world with spirit intact, if not unscathed by evil? How to negotiate the *via affirmativa* of human society without being spiritually poisoned by it. How to live well, to *grow* well. As the protagonist of "Yvonne" puts it at the story's conclusion, observing his nephews' concern over whether the crabs they are catching will experience pain when they are cooked: "I looked at the boys . . . reaching down for another crab, and I hoped they would grow well, those strong little bodies, those kind hearts" (*SF,* 121).

The clerical negation is encountered early in the story in the person of the eighth-grade teacher, Brother Thomas, who informs his class of pubescent boys that sexual pleasure is reserved for marriage; "self-abuse" is a mortal sin which bars one from communion with God and could result in hell. On the other hand, he tells the boys, receiving Communion is a source of sanctifying grace; to die with the Eucharist on one's tongue virtually guarantees immediate entrance into heaven:

> But now his eyes focused on something out the window, as though a new truth had actually appeared to him on the dusty school yard of that hot spring day. One hand rose to scratch his jaw. "In a way," he said softly, "You'd actually be doing someone a favor if you killed him when he had just received the Eucharist." (*SF,* 100)

The snigger this zany bit of fanaticism tickles out is followed at once by comprehension: this fanatic embodies our corporeal/spiritual schism—death before dishonor, body and spirit at war, death the only peace—and suggests the obverse of Hamlet's bitter refusal to kill his father's murderer while he prayed, for fear of sending him to his grave at peace with God.

The protagonist of Dubus's story, Harry, soon finds his body a battleground for that war, and he is so torn by it that he considers, for one agonized instant, mutilating himself. But as quickly as the possibility occurs to him, he rejects it and, in the inevitability of that rejection, subliminally accepts that nature, too, has its inevitabilities which, as Whitman put it, are unimpeachable as the sentiments of grass and trees: "No voices told me why. . . . I simply knew it: it is there between your legs and you do not cut it off" (*SF,* 106).

Over the years that follow, Harry continues to confess, to receive Communion; then, at nineteen, he has a love affair with a girl named Yvonne, and after that, his masturbation seems hardly more than an indulgence to him.

At this point, Harry does something surprising.

His sister, Janet—probably like most of us—makes her own rules about religion. She views the Eucharist as a sacrament of love, and only *she* can judge whether she is fit to receive it or not. For example, when she has an affair with someone who loves her, but whom she does not love, she considers herself unfit to receive the Host. She finds it unnecessary to discuss such matters with the priest. Unlike Janet, Harry decides to confront the church. He decides that he is not false enough to continue to confess something he does not believe to be a sin, nor is he willing just to let it drop away into silence and make his own rules based on solitary judgment in secret, hypocritical alienation from the administrators of his religion.

In short, he chooses action over inaction, confrontation over despair or depression or evasion. Neither Hamlet nor Prufrock, he dares disturb the universe. One Saturday in confession, after perfunctorily reporting the number of times he has indulged his private vice and telling the priest—in accordance with sacramental ritual—that he is sorry for his "sin," he realizes abruptly that he is lying, that he is not sorry, that he does not even believe it is a sin. He tells this to the priest and is refused the ritual absolution without which he is barred from the sacrament of Holy Communion. This sacrament is important to Harry, as to all practicing Catholics—for it is the ritual sacrament of renewal of the soul, the sacrament of life and of love. Not having received the pre-scribed absolution, Harry cannot bring himself to receive Communion as this would constitute a major offense against the framework of ritual within which the Catholic religion is practiced. Thus his courage to act cuts him off from the sacrament of love, from the ritual union with Christ—which, to the Catholic, is a mystical event by which the power of human belief literally transforms the substance of bread into the body of Christ—from the religion that is otherwise his sustenance, and he suffers a period of limbo. Finally, though, he tries again. He goes to another priest and tells the whole story, that he does not believe masturbating is a sin or making love is a sin, but that his sin with Yvonne was of *using* her for sex when he didn't love her and of bragging to some other boys about what he had done with her.

The object of this act of spiritual courage by Harry clearly is to maintain a direct communion with the religion into which he was baptized and through which he has communed with the sacred essence of existence and developed a moral sense strong enough to force him to stand up even against the religion itself. In response, the priest shifts the focus for Harry (and the reader) by quoting John: "I do not pray that You take them out of the world, but that You keep them from evil" (*SF,* 120). Thus, the conflict of body and spirit dissolves into a broader frame affirmative of the world, of the human power to choose good over evil.

The ritual of confession for a Catholic always ends with the assignment of a penance—a series of prayers to be uttered, deeds to be performed, contributions to be given to the poor, acts to be carried out in full letter and spirit if the ritual is to be effectively completed. In this case, the penance the priest assigns to Harry is to say "Alleluia" three times (*SF,* 120)—a religious celebration of a boy's recognition and acceptance of the naturalness of his own sexuality.

It is interesting to compare Harry Dugal with another, more celebrated onanist of the sixties: Alexander Portnoy. Both Harry and Portnoy are distressed by their acts. Both are dealing with it via confession, one to a priest, the other to an analyst. But perhaps the main difference between them is that Harry, like Poe's sailor, responds to the maelstrom into which he is drawn by studying its governing principles with a view to securing his deliverance from it; Alexander Portnoy dives headlong into the whirlpool.

7

Portnoy confesses to his Freudian psychiatrist that he has been driven mad by his mother's unconsciousness of the unconscious. Harry Dugal, like most of Dubus's characters, is not concerned with Freudian consciousness; the awareness he seeks to develop is one in which he is able to distinguish right from wrong in order to find harmony with his own spirit. Portnoy's confession ends with a page-long Janovian primal scream, Harry's with a chant of joy.

Another comparison that seems appropriate is with Roth's short story "The Conversion of the Jews," in which a child brings the whole community of his synagogue and his rabbi down onto their knees by threatening to jump off the roof if they do not admit that God's power *could* bring about a virgin birth. Harry, however, affirms sexuality within the context of a religion that previously had sought to negate its worth; the child in Roth's story performs a feat in some ways opposite to this, forcing an element of mystical innocence into the framework of a pragmatic community in which there is no place for the miraculous.

There is a kind of sublime obstinacy in the character of Harry Dugal which is, I think, the kernel about which much of Dubus's fiction crystallizes. His people know their sins, or at least sense them, look hard for some clue to where their moral knot has tangled—the "little death" of being a stranger between the thighs of a stranger ("Going Under," *SF*), of lying to simulate love, of debasing love by tapping into the darkness of its underside, as the young married couple do in Dubus's short second novel, *Voices from the Moon (VFM)*. Or, like Luke Ripley in the masterful "A Father's Story" *(TNSB)*, they must sin to preserve love and take the consequence of a debate with God for the rest of their lives. Or else, like "The Pretty Girl" *(TNSB)*, Polly Comeau, they only sense that their "life is not good, though in a way the church has never defined" for them (26).

But with the exception of a few pieces—particularly some of the military stories—written, Dubus has said, as a deliberate exploration of the lives of people spiritually unlike himself, his characters nearly always suffer a sense of moral derailment in their lives. Cynicism and indifference are not dignified by humor or irony in the fiction of Dubus, whose characters sooner or later must face the consequences of their moral and spiritual failures, if not in this story, then in the next, or the next after that, as with Hank Allison who grows through three long stories—"We Don't Live Here Anymore" *(SF)*. "Adultery" *(AOC)*, and "Finding a Girl in America" *(FGA)*—from cynical self-completeness to a love that frames the optimism of commitment to wife and children. In a *New York Times* review of Dubus's fiction, Lisa Zeidner suggests that, like Rilke, he seems to consider happiness unimportant, and it would appear that happiness is not a main concern of his work.[1] Dubus's fiction seems not to seek delight so much as the enlightenment of experience. The affirmative conclusion of "If They Knew Yvonne" is an affirmation of life, but of a life whose mysteries are sorrowful as well as joyful.

In contrast to Harry Dugal's story, two of the five Paul Clement stories focus on the failure of courage and the other three view Paul in relation to his father at three phases of his life. But one important element shared by all these stories of youth is that of betrayal—of trading love or loyalty for survival. The vision in the Paul Clement stories is dark—much darker than the ultimately joyous spiritual journey of Harry Dugal.

With "The Bully" and "Cadence" *(AOC)*, we experience an unblinking examination of some of manhood's less seemly aspects. In "An Afternoon with the Old Man" *(AOC)*, "Contrition" *(AOC)*, and "Goodbye" *(TNSB)*, we witness, through the eyes of the offspring, the quiet tragedy of disconnection between father and son. In later stories, Dubus examines the relationship from the other side, transcending the tragedy by expanding the circle of our understanding, as in "A Father's Story" *(TNSB)*, although he also deals with the rupturing of the father-child relationship in the bud of its development by divorce and geographical separation: "Going Under" *(SF)*, "At St. Croix" *(FGA)*, "The Winter Father" *(FGA)*, and others.

Perhaps one of Dubus's most powerfully disturbing stories is "The Bully," in which a child's personal degradation and his involvement in the process are unflinchingly examined. For three years, Paul Clement, now in sixth grade, has been bullied daily by an older boy named Larry, who has been repeatedly left back year after year. Each day, Paul accepts the pinches and kicks and punches with an ingratiating smile, and each night, he entertains himself before sleep with visions of Larry's humiliation.

Paul, himself, though, is no stranger to cruelty. The story opens

9

with a scene of him killing a cat, an act that is perhaps symbolic for the child who seems to view the cat as a reflection of his own cowardice and thus, perhaps, the act of killing it as a ritual killing of that aspect of himself or as a vindication of what he suffers as a result of his fear.

Nonetheless, the cruelty is performed with chill fascination, an act mirroring the cruelty that is a daily feature of Paul's life at school. He and his friend, Eddie, are depicted, both here and in "Contrition" *(AOC),* as weak boys, victims, outsiders, unable to take action against forces that stifle them. In "Contrition," the boys try, in vain, to distinguish themselves by taking up a musical instrument, an enterprise that fails but leaves Paul a glimmer of awareness about himself and his father—as Dubus refers to it, a little like Kafka winning a glimpse from his father's side of things. At the end of "Contrition," Paul realizes how little he has learned of courage in his ten years, an interesting contrast to the concluding scene of "The Bully," which leaves Paul, the victim, entertaining himself with vindictive, graphic speculations about the misfortune that has befallen the boy who has bullied him.

In "The Bully," Paul is a passive accomplice to his situation— a passivity further explored in the more recent "Rose" *(LWE),* with its first-person creative-narrator's reminiscence of a young man in officer training whose weakness is not of the body but of the spirit—a weakness that is a mystery Dubus seems to puzzle over in many of his stories: a strong body whose heart stifles its own force. What causes Rose to disconnect from her natural maternal resistance to her husband's abuse of their son? Why does Paul smile at his tormentor? Why does he not respond in kind when a reflex of loyalty on Eddie's part draws the bully's attention from Paul to Eddie? Instead, Paul tries to please the bully by admiring the effectiveness of the blow he delivers to Eddie's solar plexus—and vainly, cunningly, seeks to tempt the bully to fight another, stronger boy against whom he would have no chance.

These are reflections of the moral and spiritual complexities children face daily, the all too human reflex of cowardice which has Paul turn, at moments of trial, to deny his friend, his father, even himself. Interestingly, in "Cadence," when Paul's "manhood" finally passes the trial of Marine officer training, the courage he chooses is the "wrong" courage, a courage that forces him once again to a betrayal of friendship and of love. Here, again, Paul and Munson—like Paul and Eddie—are outsiders, weak boys struggling to survive in the society of the strong. But instead of seeking to preserve the friendship—as Munson does, with a strength that develops when his *awareness* of weakness grows into wisdom—Paul turns away from the greater physical weakness of his friend, even as Munson seeks the strength to reject what he finally has come to view as a futile exercise in virility. "Is that smart?" he demands of Paul: to run until you puke? (*AOC*, 79) Thinking that Paul's strength is giving out on a long march, Munson drops out as well, falls behind to stand with his friend in "weakness," in a recognition of the futility of what they are doing.

But Paul rallies, conquers his body, completes the march, and finally joins the platoon in ostracizing Munson for his weakness, his "inability" to complete the training program, his decision to drop out. This final betrayal of Munson by Paul, the refusal to speak to him in the mess hall, is written with skillful understatement by Dubus which saves it from even a trace of the melodrama to which military fiction can otherwise be so vulnerable; and the outcome has already been powerfully foreshadowed in a hand-to-hand combat training scene in which Paul and his friend, pitted against one another, stare into each other's eyes before Paul moves into action, abstracting himself from the fact that the body he is facing is that of his friend, Munson.

There are several common elements among these six stories—the five about Paul Clement and the one about Harry Dugal: the element of love threatened by cowardice, of betrayal of love in the interests of survival; the mystery of spiritual weakness checking physical strength; the misjointed bond of love between father and son and its relationship to the other elements.

Five of the stories hinge to a greater or lesser extent on betrayal—in "An Afternoon with the Old Man," Paul's fantasy of his father's death in its meager garb of hypocritical sorrow; in "Contrition," Paul's denial of his father at a moment of trial to shift blame away from himself; in "The Bully," Paul's denial of his friend, Eddie, as well as his abandonment of his own existence to the condition of victim who smiles at his own torment and tormentor; in "Cadence," Paul's betrayal of Munson to avoid any possible challenge to his own tenuous, newly won "manhood"; in "Yvonne," Harry's denial of Yvonne's humanity, first by the exploitation of her body, later by bragging to his classmates about it.

The story "Goodbye" seems as much a conclusion to this sequence of youth stories as "An Afternoon with the Old Man" is an opening. In the latter, Paul daydreams of his father's death as a release—a dream with clear Oedipal undertones, packaged in unconscious hypocrisy as he envisions himself praying over the grave while his girlfriend admires his piousness. The former functions on an implicit irony: Paul and his pregnant wife take leave of his father and mother and the older couple's soured marriage to move forth into their own life together—one whose commencement is a shotgun wedding. The stories in between, with one exception, are tales about the failure of love resulting from cowardice or misconceived courage. The exception, again, is "Yvonne," in which spiritual courage enables a young man to preserve the religious faith that is his sustenance.

Although numerous other stories by Dubus deal with youth and the spiritual complexities that young people must face, of human beings encountering their vulnerability for the first time in their lives and their own and others' weakness and evil, these six stories encapsulate the central image of Dubus's view of youth as the first confrontation with the existential human challenge to do more than survive. In Dubus's world, even a cat bolting from danger does so with "a wise and determined face" while a kitten, "afraid and uncertain . . . pretend[s]" that danger is not present ("The Bully," *AOC*, 24).

These children Dubus draws for us must learn a courage, wisdom, and determination greater than ever will be demanded of a cat—for they must learn to uphold the new commandment given to man by Christ: that you love one another. This is the journey of education that Paul and his pregnant wife finally embark upon at the end of this sequence of fictions, in "Goodbye," as they drive away from Paul's unhappy, aging parents and their stagnant marriage—a journey whose turnings will be traced through many of Dubus's later fictions of adult life, of violence, of marriage, of professionalism, of parenthood.

The Girls:
Who They Are

It was womanhood they were entering, the deep forest of
it, and no matter how many women and men too are
saying these days that there is little difference between us,
the truth is that men find their way into that forest only
on clearly marked trails, while women move about in it
like birds.

—Andre Dubus, "A Father's Story," *TNSB,* 166

A prominent feature of the fiction of Andre Dubus is its portrayal
of women. He calls them girls, the way they call themselves girls,
but they're women really, presented as women, even the very
young ones, most of them, and they are responsible for their lives,
for their actions, and their failures to act. Their stories are told
from their own viewpoints, sometimes first person, and their
presentation, their identity as women would seem a vital element
of the world in which Dubus's fiction occurs.

When Billy Wells's wife leaves him in "The Pitcher" *(FGA),*
the event is important to the story, but the woman who leaves
is peripheral. When Edith or Polly or Molly's mother leaves her
husband or when Terry holds onto hers, the woman is central to
the event and, in her choice of action, to the story. Edith and
Terry experience events as women which will define their men,
just as their men, by their attentions or neglect, have defined the
fates of their wives. Polly's choice of essential inaction leads to
a death, one for which she is responsible, even if she does not
recognize or assume that responsibility.

When Louise, "The Fat Girl" *(AOC),* allows herself to be badg-
ered into dieting so that she can fulfill the image expected of her
by the world, she identifies herself with a situation that provides
all the goods and pleasures she is supposed to want, but to maintain
her "worthiness" for them, she must maintain the identity that
others desire for her, one that grants her admission to the world

of things. She must not be fat. She must be slim. She must be hungry, must learn to live with a hunger that nags incessantly at her spirit, in order to satisfy the cravings of the people around her. If she will not provide them with the appearance they desire of her, they will not accord her love or, worse, will look upon her with repugnance until she "pulls herself together" and "starts taking care of her looks" again. To the world around her, she *is* how she looks: fat. That is her identity. She is a fat girl. Finally, she decides that *she* will determine her own identity.

At the opposite pole, "The Pretty Girl" *(TNSB)* is about a woman, Polly Comeau, who is unable to transcend the special treatment accorded her because of her pretty face, unable to develop a strength deeper than appearance. Polly's sin is not an act, but a lack of action, an acquiescence to the exceptions American society makes for a young good-looking woman, a failure to assume existential responsibility for herself because of moral laziness fostered by her good looks and by the way the world has responded to her surface prettiness. Her story ends with manslaughter, with a violence that reveals the pitiful depths of the woman's moral vacuity—at which many a witness might be reluctant to cast the first stone.

Violence also visits the lives of Ellen ("Andromache," *AOC*), Juanita Creehan ("Waiting," *AOC*), Leslie ("Leslie in California," *TNSB*), the unnamed rape victim of "In My Life" *(SF),* Anna ("Anna," *TNSB*), and Rusty ("Blessings," *Delta*), although each visitation has its own distinct turn and significance in defining the existence of the given character.

In "Andromache," the death of Ellen's mate comes to her as the death of Hector to his queen, a soldier's death, albeit in peacetime, experienced as the fate of the wife of man. Ellen's life, like the lives of the other wives on the military reservation, is a function of her husband's service to the nation. It is a rare year when a new widow is not made; this year it is Ellen. Her husband dies in a plane crash, and she is left at thirty-five with two children, a son who, when he grows up, "only has to die," and a nine-year-old daughter already so attuned to the conditions of her life that she knows it without having to hear the news behind the knock at the door. Like the Andromache of myth, however, Ellen's orientation clearly will continue to be toward life, the life of the military.

The Girls: Who They Are

Dubus's other military widow, Juanita Creehan, has lost her husband in combat in Korea, and life for her is defined as little more than a waiting for death, apparent in her oddly carnal attraction to the news of a former schoolmate's suicide. Juanita looks to the sea as a symbol of the oblivion that will one day be granted her, for which she waits not without a shade of welcome, perhaps not without an intention to hasten that day's arrival. The danger that touches the life of "Leslie in California" *(TNSB)* comes from her husband. In this very short story, the main character wakes with a black eye inflicted by her husband after he got drunk the night before. He has been unemployed for most of the time since they moved cross-country and has hit her now three nights in a row. They are out of money, and their electricity has been shut off. She gets up in the morning to make him breakfast before he goes off on a fishing boat where he may earn some money. In the kitchen, she fries his eggs while he blames his behavior on drink and promises her gifts, and she wonders if she will end up dead one day in her kitchen, like some corpse in the newspaper.

"In My Life" follows a woman through the day in 1956 when a man convicted of raping her is electrocuted. He is black, she is white; he had never committed any crime before, and the execution is taking place nearly two years after the rape—long after the intensity of her desire to strike back has lifted. She is divorced, a cocktail waitress who sleeps with a succession of married men. She has had eleven men in her life. She doesn't count "the nigger" who raped her, although his body had touched her and now they were burning it *(SF,* 97). Her life, in a sense, is metaphorically violated by the legal process executing the man who literally violated her. These events are a part of her life now, her fate, and she is defined by them both—the rape and the rapist's execution, which only adds to the burden of that fate.

Anna Griffin's fate, too, veers through a sector of crime. She is a counter girl at the supermarket; her common-law husband, Wayne, cooks hamburgers at Wendy's. Their little apartment is furnished with "leavings"—an old sofa, a chair, a yellow table, a mattress on the floor. They want things, all the things advertised in the magazines sold on the rack in the store where she works. So Anna waits at the wheel of the getaway car one snowy night while Wayne goes into a drugstore and steals two thousand dollars at knife-point.

They buy a television set, a stereo, records, a vacuum cleaner, and have some good times in the local bar. But their acquisitions do not bring the satisfaction they were seeking: "There's too much to get. There's no way we would ever get it all" (*TNSB*, 157). What *are* they to get, then, in this world of objects in which the young couple finds themselves? What does the world offer beyond "stereos and color televisions and soft carpets and soft furniture and large brass beds" (*TNSB*, 138) other than liquor and pills to still the pain of awareness? The submerged note of hope in this piece might be the first step in Anna's self-definition of her existence—the dawning realization that money is not the answer to spiritual vacuity.

By contrast, the violence that visits the life of Rusty ("Blessings") is a natural violence that blesses her family with a more intimate understanding of existence, of the conditions and fate of creatures framed in mortality, the biological fate as opposed to the sociological. This is discussed in more detail in the chapter on violence.

Some of Dubus's women meet their fates head-on. Edith and Terry find their own terms—each in her own way—in unsatisfying marriages: Edith by finding strength in love to stop living in a dead marriage with a man whose cynical egotism has insulated him from her; Terry by choosing the crucial moment to stand firm, to hold her family together despite the yearnings and weaknesses that have turned her husband and herself to adultery. Rose, too, finally takes action against her husband's violent mishandling of their children ("Rose," *LWE*), thus saving them from him, but she is unable to recognize in herself the further potential of strength to take over the tiller of the family.

Both "The Fat Girl" and Bobbie of "Graduation," perhaps more than any other of Dubus's women, refuse to accept the fate dealt to them as women. As a child, the fat girl is driven to secret eating by a mother who warns her that her more-than-healthy appetite will end by making her unpopular with boys: "if you're fat, the boys won't like you; they won't ask you out" (*AOC*, 45).

Louise's response to this command to accept passivity (to become an object whose fate is determined by its desirability or lack thereof, whose choices include being asked out or staying home) is to assume hypocrisy: she becomes a secret eater, gorging herself on sweets in bed at night and then nibbling salads in the school lunchroom, creating a fiction that her metabolism is responsible for her weight. But Louise "knew why she was fat; she was fat because she was Louise. . . . God had made her this way. She did not want to go around angry and hungry and thinking of food" (*AOC,* 46).

When she is alone at home, she finds her body natural and acceptable; only when she leaves the house does she begin to see herself through the eyes of others, as fat and repulsive. She chooses her friends—those other misfits whose friendship is available to her—for their slimness to avoid a situation of being paired into a twosome of fat girls, for she could not bear the thought of seeing how others might look at them.

In college, though, she makes friends with Carrie, whose friendship is deeper; Carrie discovers the secret eating and invites Louise to feel free to eat openly, to be herself. Apart from Louise's father, Carrie is the only one who has ever loved Louise for herself, without condition. Carrie then helps Louise to diet, and the genuineness of her concern inspires Louise to cooperate. For a year, she diets, or rather they diet together, Carrie guiding her through. In her hunger Louise is afflicted by ill temper, and it seems "like a demon taking possession of her soul" (*AOC,* 51). At some point, confused, she feels she is losing more than weight; she is losing herself (*AOC,* 52). The object of the diet is to make her body sufficiently presentable and attractive that she will be able to win the love of a man, that she will emerge "out of the hibernation of fat that has kept her from a love life" (*AOC,* 53).

Finally, she slims down to the agreed-upon 113 pounds, and her old friends and family accept her as a returned prodigal. Her mother pronounces her "beautiful." And "she lived at home and ate the way her mother did, and every morning she weighed herself on the scales in her bathroom" (*AOC,* 54). She wins a husband then and feeds him Italian food she herself must not eat, and they prosper, acquiring a house and a boat, and enjoying expensive vacations: "by slimming her body, she had bought into the pleasures of the nation" (*AOC,* 55) (those pleasures that Anna and Wayne had tried to acquire at knife-point).

Then she becomes pregnant, and her body begins to grow again. Her husband "requests" that she stop smoking while she is pregnant, and she does, but loses her hard-won discipline. She begins to eat again. Soon she is fat, and her husband grows impatient with her, complains, argues. Louise remembers the compassion with which Carrie had helped her. Carrie had loved *her;* her husband loves her only if she is slim. (This selective style of love appears also in "We Don't Live Here Anymore," in which Terry accuses her husband of loving actions rather than a person, "tricks . . . the fucking and spaghetti sauce" [*SF,* 60]). Louise's husband will not make love to her when she is fat, will not even touch her, and feels perfectly justified in implying to her that this is because she is disgusting to look at. She recognizes a strain of cruelty in him that she had never seen before, and she continues to eat, driving him from her life. She then claims that life for herself and her baby to do with as she sees fit, resisting the pressure to regain that slim appearance others define as worthy to behold.

There is no doubt the world does judge by surface and is cruel to those who deviate from the superficial norm, cruel to fat people, perhaps especially fat women. (This fact is also at the root of the crime in "Land Where My Fathers Died," to be discussed in a later chapter.) In "The Fat Girl," although Dubus never deviates from the surface story of superficiality, an argument could be made that he uses that surface story as a metaphor for the conflict between the painful craving of inner hungers and the need to deny them if we are to gain access to the inner circles of fulfillment in our society, to the "pleasures of the nation," the superficial trappings of love and happiness. To give rein to the inner yearnings, to deviate from the norm, is to invite rejection, to position oneself to be shunned, to be a loser and an outcast.

This is perhaps most true for women, who can win a life or lose one, on the strength of a pretty face or slender figure. In this sense, Polly Comeau and Louise are counterparts; "The Pretty Girl" and "The Fat Girl" are companion pieces about the spiritual superficiality of the American way of life.

The beautifully written "Graduation" *(AOC)* also deals with superficiality, albeit a now outdated one: the hypocritical require-ment of a male-dominated society that a bride be a virgin. In this story, Bobbie loses her virginity and, without ever quite examining the fate to which this delivers her, becomes the "other" kind of girl. All this really means is that she sleeps with three young men during her high school years, but that is enough to brand her as "a good piece," which someone writes on a picture of her and pins to the school bulletin board. The remainder of her time in high school becomes a cold, loveless period. Even her date for the high school graduation party is a young man who makes it evident that he is after easy sex.

When she goes away to college, however, she realizes that no one there knows anything about her past, and she creates a new life for herself, becomes a virgin again. She resists the physical advances of the boy who falls in love with her, and in a moment of intimacy tells him that she was once raped by an uncle. She holds him on the leash of his desire and manipulates that desire so that it leads finally to marriage. She lives a normal life now, her future protected by a gap separating it from her past. The only regret she has is the sadness of being loved without really being known, and this is the paradox of the story: if Bobbie tries to share the truth of her life, she risks losing the love that does not know her.

We find this need to be known in much of Dubus's fiction. The priest in "Adultery" leaves the church to fulfill this need, and Hank in "Finding a Girl in America" experiences the pain of not being known by his lover. This makes him realize, finally, how unkind he had been to his former wife by never caring to "know" her—an ironic turn of the biblical phrase for fornication. In Dubus's fiction, to love is to *know* the beloved, not the body so much as the private reality of his or her existence. To seek an appearance instead of a person is to seek to circumvent the pain and complexity of love.

We see this in "Molly," in which Claire's husband, Molly's father, obsessed with his work and essentially indifferent to his family, finally leaves them to embrace "the freedom of selfishness." For Claire, freedom is being able to "live each day without violating her conscience" (*LWE,* 120). This, however, is something she learns only after Norman has left her, and there is no longer any adult between her and the world. From her experience with Norman, she learns "that the desire to know another and be known by him, was futile" (*LWE,* 123). Claire strives to teach her daughter from her own experience, seeks to be wholly truthful with the girl that they might have a fullness of love. Experience, however, is nonnegotiable, and Molly's journey toward love must be a personal one. Her initiation into sex at the age of fifteen, which takes place *after* the so-called sexual revolution, is as cruel in its own way as Bobbie's early experiences at the hands of male double standards. It is a gray event, the purchase of a shallow experience at the cost of innocence, and—as the fifteen-year-old girl tries to imagine what remains for her—it points to a future of insufficiency. Here Dubus seems to present the fact that the essence of love and sexuality are constants, that every generation must learn the difference between hunger and love, each under its own specific conditions.

In "Bless Me, Father," too, we find reference to "knowing" a loved one. Here, a young girl, Jackie, discovers that her father is an adulterer and writes him an indignant letter. The father comes to visit her at her college, and she is put off balance by his apparent lack of shame at having been found out. Jackie has indicted him for the pain he has caused her mother, but the father calmly informs her that the difference between her and her mother is that his wife knows him and she, Jackie, does not. He tells her that for the sake of family peace he has ended his affair (although he indicates to her that it is more complex than sordid) and returns her letter with a request that she study it and decide whom she really wrote it for. The implication is that he *knows* her better than she knows herself—again the measure of the depth of love in Dubus's fiction.

The mystery of knowing (or *not* knowing) another person is also an important element of "His Lover" *(FGA)*, in which a young woman who initiates physical love with an elderly blind man turns out to be a cold-blooded killer. The blind man knows nothing of the girl, Linda, beyond the pleasure of her hands on his body. (This story will be explored further in the chapter dealing with violence.)

In Dubus's fiction, not to know is not to love and not to love is to proceed on the march to death alone, with the "soul untapped" ("Going Under," *SF,* 135). But for his women, a more frequent problem than not knowing the beloved is the situation of not *being* known and thus being abandoned on a kind of separate flight through life, forced into an identity of mere appearance and pragmatism.

Miranda ("Miranda over the Valley," *SF*) and Beth ("Separate Flights," *SF*) are two more of Dubus's women, the one at the beginning of her life, the other at the middle, who come up against a society that seeks to define them in terms of convenience and pragmatism. Beth and her husband, when they travel, always take separate flights to avoid the possibility of orphaning their children. On one such flight, Beth meets another man and finds herself verbally betraying her husband; she has the intention of committing adultery and realizes how easily this decision has come in the broken state of their marriage and in her disconnection from a belief in anything. When her daughter asks her advice about sex, Beth is unable to respond; she does not know, has no moral context from which to draw.

The demand made of Miranda is as elemental as can be made by society: to undergo the abortion of a pregnancy she wishes to carry to term. Her boyfriend, her parents, and her roommate all agree that it would be foolish of her to ruin her life by having a child at that point in her education, but Miranda sees herself surrounded by people for whom human relationships are a matter of convenience, or pragmatism. She does not wish to accept the dictates of that world and vainly seeks the courage to have her child. However, she too succumbs to the demands of the superficial society which she allows to define her. We see Miranda again later in "Going Under" (SF) unable to commit herself to the love that Peter Jackman wants to share with her. Ironically, Jackman is going under as a result of having been deprived of his children when his former wife moved across the country, taking them with her. But Miranda has been too damaged by her past to recognize or to accept the quality of a love she had earlier sought, but had been driven to turn from. Finally, she is unable to know Jackman or to see in his pain the reflection of the person she once had wished to be.

In *Voices from the Moon,* the attempt by Brenda to know her husband and to share his reality leads them to the dark language of desire. When Larry proposes that they act out his voyeuristic fantasies, Brenda's response is immediate: I'll do that for you. There follows a series of bar pick-ups in which Larry and Brenda conduct a scenario: Larry feigns drunkenness, pretends to go to bed, and leaves his wife alone with the man they have invited home with them that evening; then, while Brenda seduces the man, Larry watches through the keyhole on his knees. But this is only one section of the book. Worthy of further exploration is the fact that when Larry and Brenda ultimately part, Brenda ends up with Larry's father. What are the implications for Brenda as a character in these strange events? Is she, in fact, locked into a pattern in the life of a person not herself, playing a secondary role in the Oedipal complex of her ex-husband, or does her participation in the play lead her from immature to mature love?

The questions of identity and knowing and being known are bound together. Obviously, a person who lacks a clear identity will be deprived of the possibility of being deeply known and loved and will perhaps also be incapable of knowing another fully or offering love's comfort. Thus Beth, lacking identity, does not know what to tell her daughter about sex. Claire fails to differentiate fully between her daughter Molly and herself, sees the girl as an opportunity to correct her own mistakes rather than as an individual in her own right, with her own specific needs. By trying to *give* her an identity that is a reflection of her own past failures, she denies the girl the identity that might have evolved naturally. Claire tries to love, but fails because in stripping off her old identity, her old values, she has failed to define adequately her new ones.

In Dubus's fiction, particularly in his treatment of female characters, we find this continuing focus and refocus on the question of a character's defining her or his own identity juxtaposed against the identity a situation seeks to impose upon the character. Larry's mother, Joan, finally gives it words toward the end of *Voices from the Moon*. Separated from Larry's father, she lives alone and works as a waitress in the heart of the lower-middle-class New England where the bulk of Dubus's fiction takes place. Joan has found herself here, in a life of small details, of daily communications. She tells her son what she has learned from that existence: that it is not necessary to live a great life, that life itself is enough.

Thus, in Dubus's fiction about women, we find central questions of identity and intimate human communication. The items of everyday life upon which Dubus focuses count for *all* here, for he finds his metaphors—as Flannery O'Connor urged—in the element in which his characters, and, presumably, his readers, live daily. The meaning of the events are within the events, part and parcel of them. What the characters experience is what they are; their fate *is* them. The fate of his women is in their womanhood. To paraphrase Hemingway's comment on what he saw as the excessive symbolic explication of his *Old Man and the Sea:*

the girls are girls, their lives lives, nothing more and nothing less. In the details of their daily lives, in their relationships to the people, objects, and events of which their days are composed, Dubus's women unfold as characters and are defined, either actively or passively.

And, once again, action or inaction is often the key to identity in Dubus's fiction, not least for his women. This, of course, is the existential challenge: to define oneself or to be defined. In one way or another, each of Dubus's women face this challenge, essentially a challenge to self-knowledge as a stage in the bridging of human isolation, or in succumbing to it, in being lost to hunger, or progressing beyond hunger to love as a higher state of existence.

Some of Dubus's women do not make it to that state, but a few do. And this would seem to be the way in which humanity goes beyond mere survival to prevail in the world of Dubus's fiction. This is the triumph available—a triumph over loneliness and ignorance of one's own nature, the possibility of knowing oneself and others which constitutes the complex of experience we call love.

The fact that Dubus chooses, in many cases, to explore this theme through female characters is not difficult to comprehend, for it would seem to be in the *appearance* of women—the pretty face or the fat body—that the experience of love in Dubus's America has snarled into a knot which the deft fingers of his prose work to untangle.

Stories of Military Life:
The Compartmentalization of Sex

A professional soldier, that is what I felt like. . . . I didn't
have a conflict about being a Marine and an artist. At that
time, I thought that writers were very good people, sort
of chosen angels. This is an idea I'm still trying to get rid
of.

—Andre Dubus

Many powerful moments in the fiction of Dubus are related to
his characters' military experiences. In "At St. Croix" *(FGA)*, Peter
Jackman, divorced and deprived of his children, of the opportunity
to fulfill his responsibility for them, experiences a terror of the
water; yet he recalls how as a Marine infantry officer responsible
for a platoon of men, he leaped into the sea in full battle gear
and led their swim to shore. In "Rose" *(LWE)*, the narrator recalls
an incident in officer training school which is a key to understanding the spiritual weakness portrayed in the story.

But these are only moments, strands in the greater patterns of
the stories. A number of Dubus's stories take place entirely in
military settings. This is perhaps not surprising considering that
he was an officer in the U.S. Marine Corps for nearly six years.
He was, in his own words, a professional soldier, and his military
fiction reflects a professional's viewpoint although without the
obsessive military focus of a writer like James Jones and without
a focus on war (Philip Caputo, Norman Mailer) or on exclusively
military problems such as the moment of command as handled,
for example, by Wouk in *The Caine Mutiny* or by Conrad in the
seminal event at the beginning of *Lord Jim*. A sort of Kiplingesque
concern for the soldier's lot is apparent in a number of these
military stories, although Dubus's characters need no Atkins or
Deever refrains to win our sympathy and respect. Young men
with large burdens, they earn respect on their own two feet.

Many of the stories that come under this military grouping,

24

however, need not occur in a military setting, although the setting does serve the thematic intentions well. But because their central concerns are not intrinsic to the military life, I deal with them in other chapters. "Cadence," discussed in the first chapter, is a story of youth and maturation and survival at the cost of loyalty. "Deaths at Sea," a story of racial hatred, fear, mistrust, and pride dividing men united in a common purpose, has more to do with violence in America than with military life per se and thus is included in the chapter on violence, along with "Dressed Like Summer Leaves," a powerful story about our inexcusable innocence of what really happened in Vietnam. "Andromache" and "Waiting" seem more about women as women than as military widows, and therefore, they are included in the chapter discussing Dubus's women. "The Captain," a story about a retired Marine Corps officer who has survived two wars, taking leave of his son who is about to ship out for Vietnam, seems to me more focused on the subject of fatherhood than on the military and is accordingly discussed under that theme.

What remains for discussion in this chapter, therefore, are five stories dealing with different aspects of a common theme: the compartmentalization and desocialization of sex and the consequent erosion of commitment between human beings. The military setting is a most likely one for this theme, providing an essentially desexualized community in which to explore it, a society where sex is something that occurs beyond the perimeters of community rather than as an intrinsic part of life, yet which affects—at times profoundly—the durability of the human relationships comprising that society.

When the wife of a sailor who goes to sea to defend his country amuses herself with the cynical first sergeant of the Marine barracks who, in turn, gives her away to one of his men for his own greater amusement, we are witnessing at least two layers of meaning. On the one hand, this suggests a kind of Chaucerian celebration of vulgarity or eroticism blind to moral consequence, revelling in its comic outrageousness as in the Miller's or Summoner's tales. On the other, it entails the undermining of social trust to a degree that can short-circuit contact with the most basic of human values: a respect for life that outweighs less substantial considerations, that makes of a man "a better human being than his nature wants to be" (to cite one of Dubus's influences, William Faulkner).

The Short Fiction: A Critical Analysis

The theme is most fully developed in the disturbing study of homosexuality and society's reaction to it portrayed in "The Dark Men" *(FGA)*. "The Misogamist" *(FGA)* treats the theme from another angle, professionalism versus family life (a little like the concerns of "The Pitcher" *[TNSB]*, where the profession, however, is not soldiering, but baseball, and the professional dedication more lyrical and mythic in its isolating effect. Dubus's presentation of the pitcher is lyrical and the lyricism elevates the essentially trivial subject to a metaphor for the mythic contest of a man struggling to master his natural imperfection). In a number of ways, "The Misogamist" serves as an interesting companion piece to "The Dark Men," providing some illuminating comparisons and contrasts to the latter.

"The Shooting" *(AOC)* and "Corporal of Artillery" *(AOC)* deal with the pressures of family responsibility in a military setting from the point of view of young fathers. In the former story, the theme of fragmentation is further illustrated by telling the story through a series of reports and viewpoints. "Over the Hill" *(SF)* is about the dear-John desperation of a young husband separated by service from his wife.

Of the five stories, two—"Corporal of Artillery" and "Over the Hill"—deal more or less head-on with the theme and as such have a less powerful final effect. In "Over the Hill," a young Marine Corps private in Japan learns that his wife has cheated on him; he goes AWOL, is court-martialed and sentenced to three months, and makes an attempt on his life. But like the broken-hearted persona of the Peggy Lee song, "Is That All There Is?" he thought he would die, but he didn't; he chooses survival, life, responsibility over the nothingness of death.

In "Corporal of Artillery," young Corporal Fitzgerald, twenty-two years old and married with three children and more than his share of debt, reenlists—deciding the course of the remainder of his life—for the bonus that will redeem him from what he owes on a four-year-old car, an unneeded encyclopedia, an overexercised charge account, and the hospital bills for his twenty-year-old wife's nervous breakdown. Fitzgerald's troubles stem from the exercise of passion without birth control. Now they have the pill, but passion has already begun to show signs of flagging, and he is committed to a career in the corps, twenty years, carrying the responsibility for four other human beings on his young back.

But Fitzgerald's triumph, the triumph of the story, is his tough-minded acceptance of his fate. He is an impressive, responsible young man, a complete person managing both his profession and his family life. The remaining three stories under discussion in this chapter focus on the lack of that completeness and the frightening consequences of that lack.

Perhaps the strongest of the five stories discussed here, "The Dark Men" builds upon an actual incident,[2] as does the baseball story "After the Game" *(LWE)*, but the true life models on which the stories are based develop via the fiction into statements greater than the incidents themselves, dramatic as they may have been. In "After the Game," we see something of the way in which commercialism in sport uses individuals without regard for their human needs. In "The Dark Men," we find a powerful, subtle depiction of the consequences of a lack of integration of sexuality in everyday life, "images of night and shame" *(FGA,* 24) which separate us from others rather than uniting humankind in the common passion that is its continuance and one of its most positive existential expressions.

The story does not belabor the theme, though. On the contrary, it is barely touched as the story unfolds, telling itself. Intelligence officers Foster and Todd appear in "dark civilian clothes" on Captain Ray Devereaux's aircraft carrier with a file of damning information about Commander Joe Saldi, an ace pilot and the captain's friend for many years. Without ever stating it directly, the story indicates that Saldi is homosexual. Foster and Todd, "men who looked for the dark sides of other men" *(FGA,* 21), are there to force his resignation from the navy. They offer the sealed packet of evidence to the captain, who refuses to examine it and stalls long enough to be certain that Saldi is off the ship, out of reach of the dark men. Then he goes ashore to invite Saldi to lunch so that he can tell him what has happened. They have lunch and talk lightly, recalling through the spice of humor acts of valor performed by brother officers: "They did not tell stories of valor without humor, as though valor was expected, but humor was not, and the man who had both was better" *(FGA,* 28).

The captain struggles against his fear of telling Joe, but he finally does so and instantly feels the death of their friendship occur in the telling. He takes leave of his friend then, giving him the opportunity to go up in the plane he had checked out and crash it into the sea. Later, when the dark men return to the ship, the captain is standing on the deck, imagining his friend's agony as the plane dove into the water. The dark men are angry. " 'You let him fly? In a million dollar—' " (*FGA*, 30), but the captain stops them with a glance, walks away from them, and stands looking out to sea as the sun goes down and the water turns black.

The story is executed through the captain's stream of perception, but with a minimum of introspection. The perceptions occur superficially, on the surface of his consciousness, a flattish registration of the men and objects outside of Captain Devereaux. Only occasionally does the captain become consciously aware of something—of the fact that the dark men distinguish themselves from him, free themselves of his position of authority by not wearing uniforms; of the fact that one of his men is hung over; of the fact that he is unconsciously flirting with a Japanese waitress which, in turn, makes him aware that "either age or responsibility or both had this year kept him clean" (*FGA*, 25).

Twice in the story he becomes aware of some hidden knowledge in himself, some unexamined, unsurfaced information. When the two intelligence officers appear and speak Joe's name to him, "he had known what was coming next and though he had been Joe's friend for thirteen years this was the first time he knew that he knew it" (*FGA*, 24).

Thus, the captain, beneath the surface of his consciousness, has known and accepted Joe's homosexuality all along, even while the navy's bureaucracy has men out circulating to investigate and discover such irregularities. Once the information surfaces in the captain's consciousness, the innocent acceptance turns to "images of night and shame" which he must "cast . . . out." Another piece of unconscious information surfaces later, after he has taken leave of his friend: "that he knew Joe wasn't coming back, and then at once he knew he had already known that too, had known in the Club that Joe's isolation was determined and forever" (*FGA*, 29–30).

Clearly Foster and Todd are the generators of death here—even their names together can be read as such (the verb for "nurse," the German for "death"—but why does the information they bring in a sealed envelope succeed in destroying the thirteen-year friendship between the captain and Joe? Why does it lead to the captain's abandoning Joe to his suicide? Why does the captain leave Joe in the restaurant, allowing himself to remain in the dark about what he later realizes he had already known: that Joe will kill himself?

The story begins with an image of darkness—the "dark civilian clothes"—and ends with an image of darkness—"the sea darkened until finally it was black" (*FGA*, 30). The captain is troubled by Foster's and Todd's civilian clothes: " 'It's strange to talk to you gentlemen; you don't wear ribbons. I have no way of knowing where you've been.' " By contrast, Joe appears "wearing whites . . . four rows of ribbons under the gold wings on his breast" (*FGA*, 25).

The implication is that it is clear to all where Joe has "been"— militarily. Now we know something of his other life as well. Or do we? All we actually know is that two intelligence officers have come with a sealed envelope and the intention of driving Joe out of the navy. But what exactly has Joe done? We are told only that "three months ago, during a confession in San Francisco, someone gave them Joe Saldi's name" (*FGA*, 21) and that consequently the intelligence officers investigated and discovered something about Joe. Yet the information they discovered remains with them alone, for the captain does not listen to what they tell him, does not look into the envelope. Nonetheless, he has his impressions of "images of night and shame," this captain for whom the avoidance of extramarital sex is something that keeps one "clean" (*FGA*, 25).

Neither the captain nor the reader overtly knows what Joe has done. We have only our own suppositions of it, supported by the implications of the words "confession" and "San Francisco." We know from the author's own comments that the story is about a homosexual, but what in the story, itself, actually tells us this? In fact, nothing. The only words to guide us are those mentioned above together with phrases like "the dark sides of other men" and the fact that the captain realizes he has always *known* whatever it was that has been disclosed about Joe and tells that it does not matter to him and "never *did*" [*FGA*, 29]. And there are those "images of night and shame" which the captain must cast from his mind and memory. Thus, the reader must fill in gaps, must respond to implication, must consider and decide what the story is about. After all, Joe's crime could conceivably be es-

29

pionage, say, or some other sexual misdemeanor—involvement with minors or children, sadomasochistic acts or transvestitism. But somehow we know that the issue is simply his homosexuality. We do *not* know whether he is promiscuous (it is perhaps implied by the envelope, the investigation), although we *do* know that the captain has at least in the past engaged in extramarital sex and that for the past year he has been "clean." We know that the captain flirts with waitresses and has a photograph of his wife on his desk.

What actually is the story here? It seems largely to take place in the dark. Naval intelligence discovers that an officer is homosexual and reports this to the captain of his ship. The captain stalls long enough to warn the officer and give him the opportunity to commit suicide. It is a little bit like leaving a man alone in a room with a Luger and an accusation. Why does the captain act in the way that he does? Why does he not more aggressively seek to support his friend instead of leaving the way clear for him to finish himself? The answer would seem to lie in the few internal glimpses we get of the captain. To avoid extramarital sex with waitresses is to be "clean"—not "faithful" or "honest" or "loyal," but "clean." His imaginings of Joe's actions evoke for him "images of night and shame" which he must "cast out"—a term used for the exorcism of devils. To the captain, despite his professions of friendship and of not caring and never having cared, "Joe's isolation was determined and forever" (*FGA,* 30).

But why is this so *now,* only after the situation that has already existed for at least the past thirteen years has been revealed and written up in the files? Apparently Joe was not isolated before; he had his ribbons and his wings, his valor and his humor, even though the captain knew then what he was, albeit unconsciously.

Taking that knowledge from the darkness of his unconsciousness into the light of awareness, then, has cost nothing less than everything for Joe. Now his isolation is "determined and forever." The captain's only concession is not to intercede against Joe's taking a million-dollar airplane with him, thus giving his suicide some sort of special mark—glamor? machismo? Conceivably, the officer has access to a hand weapon, a .45, say, and could kill himself that way. But no, he chooses—and the captain allows him—to plunge in his plane into the darkness of the "hard and yielding sea" (*FGA,* 30).

Thus, the captain is one of the principals in Joe's death as well. Foster and Todd are not the only dark men here; the captain, too, bears his share of darkness: his knowledge of what Joe is could be borne only in the dark of unconsciousness; when he leaves Joe to his suicide he knows that he is doing it, but again only in the dark of his unconscious; when he imagines what Joe has done, he brings up images of "night and shame." Furthermore, he works at keeping himself "from thinking about what had happened in his heart this morning when, as soon as Foster spoke Joe's name, he had known what was coming" (*FGA*, 24). All are indications of a darkness of thought, an eclipse of understanding. He rages at Joe's "other face [which] he had never seen, impassioned and vulnerable in the night," although he admits to himself that he has known about it, without knowing.

The change that takes place between the two friends in this story hardly seems based on substance so much as on surface. That which is kept in the dark is permitted even if known; let the light in on it, though, and the only solution is death. What real substantive difference is there between Joe's presumably casual homosexual activity (if Joe had had a stable relationship, he might have had someone to turn to instead of committing suicide) and the captain's past flings with waitresses or whoever? This is a question the captain never asks himself; this would be an active exploration of the darkness in this story, something the captain will not undertake, for he can live with the situation only as long as it remains in the dark. When it surfaces, it threatens the clean military order through which Devereaux has ascended to the captain's bridge and is on his way to an admiralship (*FGA*, 24). Apparently Joe is *not* unconscious of what matters here, despite the captain's protestations. When Devereaux says to his friend, "I don't give a good Goddamn and I never *did*. You hear me, Joe?" Saldi's response is: " 'I hear you, Captain' " (*FGA*, 29): not name, but rank; not person, but career.

Thus, the irony in the captain's statement to Todd and Foster—"I have no way of knowing where you've been"—lies in the illumination they bring of Joe's dark side to the captain's unconscious. They show him where Joe has been, force an understanding which the military structure and his career cannot bear. Apparently, although his actions are not consciously cynical, the captain's career will fare better under the smudge of a lost plane than it would in the presence of a living homosexual friend. Ignorance, unconsciousness, fear of the dark, of the devils of shame comprise the greater darkness of this story about compartmentalization in modern life.

Sexual compartmentalization is also intrinsic to the theme of "The Misogamist," the story of a man unable or unwilling to commit himself to a family life beyond the Marine Corps. Sheila Russell has been waiting eight years in Marshall, Texas, for Staff Sergeant Roy Hodges to marry her. Hodges sees her and makes love to her every time he comes home on leave; he has proposed to her and told her she could tell her family, but he stalls. In the face of Sheila's mother, he sees an accusation that makes him feel "that God and time, life and death, were on her side; that he was a puny and defenseless man who had committed a sin of Old Testament proportion, the kind of sin you never escaped from, no matter where you went, or how long you stayed there" (*FGA*, 55). Time passes. Hodges continues to stall. He begins to find it difficult even to imagine himself married: "during the hours of his work he did not need Sheila, or anyone female. It was at night that he missed her, in the compartment smelling of male sweat and shoe polish and leather; that was when he wrote to her. When he was in port, on liberty, he did not miss her at all; he thought of her, usually after drinking and whoring, with paternal tenderness; and he sent her gifts, knowing they were junk, knowing he was incapable of buying gifts for a woman anyway, incapable of understanding their affinity for things which couldn't be used" (*FGA*, 52–53). (In "The Winter Father," this suggestion of a woman being needed or wanted for only a segment of the day also appears: "he did not even want a woman except at day's end, and had borne all the other hours of woman-presence only to have her comfort as the clock's hands moved through their worst angles of the day" [*FGA*, 118]).

As time passes, Hodges becomes more involved in the life of the corps. He goes to war and learns of death and survives and comes home and arranges for leave to get married, but doesn't show. He leaves Sheila standing at the altar. His first sergeant congratulates Hodges for his decision (in a speech that is no doubt the reason for the statement Dubus attributes to his friend Richard Yates that the story is one of the ugliest he has ever read) and fixes him up with the wife of another man, who is off to sea.

Death and marriage, the first sergeant lectures Hodges, are two holes to avoid. Hodges goes off with the woman and learns that the first sergeant encourages her to tell about her experiences with other men, and will be asking about the details of her meeting with Hodges. Hodges finds he doesn't care. He does what he came to do—uses her for relief.

Later, he tries to write to Sheila to apologize, explain, but he is unable to complete the letter. "The phone wouldn't do either. What he needed was to see her . . . to firmly and lovingly squeeze her hand and look into her eyes and then disappear, like a love-rooted ghost making its farewell" (*FGA*, 63). (We get a brief, oblique glimpse of Hodges again, years later as a sergeant-major in "Waiting," from the point of view of a woman who wakes with him in her bed and has to think before she can remember his name [*FGA*, 92]: the fate Hodges has chosen for himself.)

Some of the obscene observations made by the first sergeant in this story—by obscene I mean essential, wanton disrespect for women—are interesting in comparison to the never clarified "obscenities" implied about Joe Saldi in "The Dark Men." The first sergeant of "The Misogamist" counsels Hodges to avoid

> the hole between the legs of a woman who's wearing the fuck-ring. Unless it has been placed on her finger by some other dumb son of a bitch who figured in order to fuck self-same lady he had to get a job and buy a house to do it in. I've had many adventures in the fuck-houses of others. . . . I have never known a woman who gave a fart whether she was married or not once it came upon her that what she wanted to do was fuck. . . . I am right now . . . fucking the sweet wife of a gunner's mate stationed on a destroyer. . . . There is a color photograph of him in uniform . . . on the bureau in the bedroom, which allows him to watch my ass-end doing its humble work on his wife (*FGA*, 61–62).

Here, of course, is a kind of traditional military cynicism with regard to sex, the cynicism of men without women, men who must endure long periods without sex, who content themselves with the services of whores to still their hunger for the act of love. Thus, again, the military setting gives Dubus the thematic "place" in which to portray the compartmentalization of sex, a theme that further unites these stories with the greater themes developed in the trilogy of long stories dealt with in the chapter on marriage and divorce in his work.

There is a kind of holism to Dubus's writing about love not frequently encountered in contemporary fiction. Other male writers portraying love and marriage—Fowles, Updike, Cheever—tend to represent women as objects of beauty and pursuit. Dubus is more concerned with the question of love's unity once the pursuit is over and done, when the more complex problems of becoming a whole human being begin. As Dubus himself expresses it: "Roy Hodges, the professional Marine . . . cannot give completely of himself and become a whole man . . . [can] be an excellent professional man, but [can]not take on the obligations and responsibilities of being a complete man, and assuming a woman and a family and all that that entails" (see p. 96).

One does not know precisely the nature of Joe Saldi's behavior in "The Dark Men," but it is difficult to imagine him behaving in a manner more obscene than that which Roy Hodges's first sergeant professes to endorse. The difference between them is the subject of their behavior: the first sergeant's promiscuity is likely to be viewed by the military community with amused tolerance, humor, perhaps even some admiration, while Joe Saldi's behavior, even were it of the highest spiritual or moral quality, must not see the light of day without immediate evocations of censure and shame and invitations to suicide.

In "The Shooting" *(AOC)*, we find another bachelor sergeant who helps himself to the wives of comrades at sea—Sergeant Chuck Everett, a Marine Corps M.P. at the Naval Air Station of Whidbey Island. Everett is having an affair with Toni, whose husband is away on a carrier in the Pacific. Everett, sergeant of the guard, is on duty one night when a sailor named Korsmeyer "goes berserk," tries to cut his wrists, menaces his wife with a kitchen knife, and, disturbed by Everett's patrol truck while preparing to commit suicide, opens fire on the sergeant.

What consequently occurs comes to us via a series of reports— the local newspaper story, third-person plural hearsay ("The sailor, they said afterward, had always been funny" [*AOC*, 97]), the senior medical officer's opinion that Korsmeyer "had probably had a passive-aggressive reaction to service life in general and to his new role as a husband and nascent father" (*AOC*, 97), the written report of the investigation ("original and five copies"), and the points of view of both Everett and Korsmeyer.

The story that evolves out of this collage of fragments is a juxtaposition of one young man, buckling under a psychic strain perhaps brought on by the pressure of increasing responsibility for his family, killed by another with no responsibilities beyond his job, no family, and a girlfriend who is another man's responsibility. The killing occurs ostensibly in the line of duty; the investigation concludes that "in the heat of battle, Sergeant Everett did not hear Captain Melko's order to cease fire" (*AOC*, 98). But in fact, Everett shoots Korsmeyer unnecessarily in a state of determination to do so—Korsmeyer has already thrown down his rifle and, choking on tear gas, signaled his readiness to give up.

Everett is accorded a certain heroic status for what he has done, and he collects copies of the newspaper with his page-one photograph, gathering them stealthily from around the base, too proud to reveal his vanity, yet too vain to refrain from gathering them. He admires his picture there, "the peaceful silence" of his face photographed shortly after having killed Korsmeyer, holding the rifle he killed him with. But the peacefulness in the photo seems to be the last of Everett's peace for some time to come. At the story's end, months later, we leave Everett again handling the newspapers, over and over, now "faded yellow as in sickness" (*AOC*, 105).

Nothing is spelled out, but a conclusion might be drawn, particularly in light of Dubus's thematic concerns, from the backgrounds of the two principal characters. Korsmeyer is *not* a professional; he is a family man due for discharge in a year. He is troubled by nightmares of being buried alive. The senior medical officer—who apparently never saw Korsmeyer alive—concludes on the basis of written reports about the incident that Korsmeyer's behavior is related to the stress of service life and family responsibility. Everett *is* a professional, seven years in service, with no family; he lives alone: "The other two sergeants were married, so he shared his room with no one" (*AOC*, 104).

Why is Everett so eager to kill Korsmeyer? Was it "the heat of battle"? Perhaps. But perhaps the story is also a statement about professional conduct untempered by the trials of personal responsibility to other human beings. From a moral point of view, Everett might be said to have murdered Korsmeyer. From where the reader stands, it appears that Everett sees Korsmeyer throw down his rifle and wave his surrender, yet Everett stands up and fires three or four additional rounds, killing the sailor with bullets in the chest and throat. Korsmeyer's behavior is haunted by the devils of nightmare images and voices, yet even in his madness, he shows moral tendencies never evident in the portrayal of Everett. Korsmeyer regrets having slashed at his wife; he wishes she would return, realizes she won't, wishes that he could be freed of his nightmares and resume responsibility for the family life and civilian job that would have been his on discharge, realizes he cannot, despairs, and would likely have killed himself to break free of his network of psychic agony had the flashing light of Everett's patrol van not interrupted him. From the reader's point of view, Everett's behavior is more chilling, less comprehensible than Korsmeyer's. Korsmeyer is in agony, driven; Everett acts with an utter lack of responsibility at the crucial moment, and the military establishment decides to ignore that behavior, interpreting it in a way that makes it excusable.

Korsmeyer finally is the victim here. The world in which he lives is too fragmented, too compartmentalized to deal with his eruption of madness, even relatively mild and potentially manageable as it is. He falls victim to the vanity of Sergeant Everett in a world more interested in surface than in the deadly gaps between the fragments that compose the surface appearance of a responsible world run by responsible men. One might even consider Korsmeyer's nightmare of being buried alive as a sane psychic reaction to a milieu that is less than sane. Finally, the dreams did, in a sense, come true.

If Korsmeyer is a victim, perhaps Everett is an instrument of a society not interested in dealing with the misfit; the doctor dismisses Korsmeyer with a diagnosis, and the military establishment rubber-stamps the young man's "execution" by the sergeant of the guard. The Korsmeyers of this world short-circuit and are taken out of play. The Everetts continue to function, holding together the seams of a fiction whose implications—beneath Dubus's quiet reportage of event and experience, of act and consequence—are terrifying. Is Dubus telling us our unwritten code is that those who cannot fit in are fit to be shot? That our society is too fragmented to countenance those who buckle under compartmentalization? Is this the code to which the young Marine sergeant fell prey?

Violence:
The Language of Isolation

I do not think my own consciousness is violent. I think
if I lived in Canada or Denmark, I probably wouldn't
write much violence. I think it is mostly a reflection of
American consciousness. . . . I can't read the paper, even
the local one, without coming across violence.

—Andre Dubus

Dubus's fourth collection of stories, *The Times Are Never So
Bad,* is introduced by an epigraph from Flannery O'Connor: "The
man in the violent situation reveals those qualities least dispen-
sable in his personality, those qualities which are all he will have
to take into eternity with him."

The first story Dubus published, as a twenty-six-year-old Marine
captain, "The Intruder," was about a boy who shoots his sister's
boyfriend under ambiguous circumstances.[3] And the most recent
at this writing, "The Curse" (*Playboy,* January 1988), written
twenty-four years later, is about a gang rape, an exploration of
the greater spiritual consequences for the bystander who witnesses
an extreme act of violence.

No fewer than twenty-three of Dubus's half a hundred stories
have violent themes or subjects: racial violence, family violence,
sexual violence, violence against or by children, murder, homicidal
revenge, suicide, armed robbery, and natural violence—"nature
and her remorseless killing."[4]

Again, however, in many of these stories, violence is only
secondary to the central theme, a symptom of the greater condition
of human isolation and disconnection in a modern America structured on superficial values. Some of these stories have been dealt
with earlier. In "Anna," for example, the crime serving as the
story's fulcrum is only circumstantial to the central focus on a
young girl's yearning for identity in a world obsessed with the
display and acquisition of material goods. One of the most violent

37

of the stories, "The Pretty Girl," is also concerned with the identity, or lack of identity, of the young female protagonist, Polly Comeau; the violence in the story is largely a consequence of her moral vacuity and emotional disconnection: when finally, out of fear, she shoots her ex-husband, she phones not an ambulance but her father and lets Raymond bleed to death. The implications of the violent events portrayed in "The Shooting" also indicate that the violence results from a lack of essential emotional connection between human beings.

Of other stories discussed earlier, "The Dark Men," "Over the Hill," and "Waiting" all deal with suicide—accomplished, failed, or anticipated—and "A Father's Story" concerns hit-and-run manslaughter and a father's covering up of a serious crime by his daughter at great personal moral cost. "The Bully" depicts a child's violence against an animal and the violence of children against each other, and "Leslie in California" tells of an unemployed man's violence against his wife after they have moved far away from their hometown and from the family network. All in one way or another deal with violence as a consequence of emotional or moral disconnection, a matter central to Dubus's overall vision.

The ten stories of violence not primarily covered in other chapters also are related to this central vision, but the violence is a more intrinsic part of their themes. Some of the stories dealt with elsewhere, such as the powerful long story "Rose," display a thematic multiplicity that calls for study of their various aspects from several points of consideration and thus will be discussed here as well.

In "Killings" *(FGA),* Matt Fowler murders the young man who has killed his son, in order to spare his wife the sight of the killer walking the streets of the town while he awaits trial. Fowler's son had been involved with Dick Strout's ex-wife, and Strout shot him to death; now Strout, out on bail, has another girlfriend and a job and drinks on weekends in a bar owned by Fowler's best friend. Sometimes when Ruth Fowler goes into the local store to shop, she bumps into the man who shot her twenty-one-year-old son in the face. At night, Fowler holds his wife while she cries in the dark. He carries a gun with him in case a confrontation should arise that would give him the excuse to kill Strout. But the waiting is too much. Finally, with the help of his friend, he abducts Strout, drives him out to the woods, and kills him.

When Fowler fires at the younger man, "the explosion of the shot surrounded him, isolated him in a nimbus of sound that cut him off from all his time, all his history, isolated him standing absolutely still on the dirt road. . . . The second shot seemed to be happening to someone else, someone he was watching" (*FGA,* 18). When Fowler returns home after he and his friend have buried Strout's body, his wife is waiting for him in the dark bedroom. She knows, without having been told, what he has done, and she tries to make love to him while he relates the details, but he cannot make love, for he has isolated himself by his act. The final irony occurs when they realize they will be unable to tell their other children about it, that the children will believe their brother's murderer has escaped trial and punishment and has run off. Thus, we see the first consequence of Fowler's unnatural act, the profound isolation he must suffer for it. Even his sob at the close of the story is one of isolation, "silent in his heart" (*FGA,* 21).

The story's point is clear: the blade of murder cuts both ways. Victim and killer are united and isolated, one in death, the other in the ultimate breach of respect for human life. Like Cain, the killer has distinguished himself from humankind and presumably must suffer that distinction for the rest of his days. An intriguing question that follows from the story is whether the act of murder affects all men equally. Will a person of inferior morality suffer equally with a person of more sensitive humanity like Matt Fowler? Throughout Fowler's abduction of Strout, he must fight to prevent himself from witnessing Strout's humanity, must forbid him from speaking lest he become too close to the sound of his voice, must prevent himself from smelling the man's smells. When, finally, he must lie to Strout to accomplish the abduction, giving the younger man hope that he is not to be killed, Fowler suffers for his cruelty. Thus, there is not even a moment's satisfaction of vengeance for Fowler; his is a rational act, an extermination to eliminate Strout from their world and end Ruth's pain. Strout, presumably, killed Fowler's son in passion. It is interesting to compare the two acts and to compare the fate of suffering attached to each.

A profound lifelong isolation awaits Fowler as a result of his act of premeditated murder. It is intriguing to consider what Strout's fate might have been had he stood trial and gone to prison for his act. The suggestion is that Strout was a man of inferior morality, the son of an affluent family who pampered him, a violent husband. Might the culmination of his weakness in murder and the suffering imposed on him for it, the experience of finally having to account for his actions, have resulted in his moral development and growth?

What then, finally, is the meaning for human society of Fowler's homicidal revenge? We understand Fowler. We follow him through his deed not without the desire for him to complete it, to succeed, to rid the world of this killer. We note his reluctance, his moral hesitation, the morality he must overcome, and we urge him, on some level, to overcome it. Once he has begun the action, abducted Strout, we know he *must* complete it, even if we share his mixed feelings about the choice he has made. Yet what is the final result for the world? Strout is eliminated, but Fowler is left morally wounded to walk the earth, and his suffering will spread, has already begun to spread to his children.

If the revenge murder of "Killings" aggravates an imbalance, throwing murder upon murder, the killing in "Townies" is the result of one. Michael, a poor town boy, kills Robin, a rich college girl who has been keeping him. She decides to cut him off so that she can try to regain possession of her fate by freeing herself from drugs and alcohol and empty sex. Drunk and desperate at the prospect of having to return to his dismal room in town, Michael strikes her with his fist, does it again, cannot stop, and punches and kicks her to death. Fleeing, he relives memories of their time together and seems at last to come to terms with his act and to welcome the punishment that awaits him. He imagines himself "dead with her" (*FGA*, 47), imagines himself in an embrace of death with the girl's body, lying in the snow where he has left it.

Apart from the moral isolation he must suffer for what he has done, there is perhaps a sense of hope that in time he may come to terms with his act, may by suffering for what he has done be expiated of guilt for it. In the mindless rage of killing the girl, he has perhaps burst through the boundaries of his unconscious existence to a reality in which he might achieve, by his conscious acceptance of the suffering resulting from his crime, a greater humanity.

The story is not only about this act of murder, though. The story is about societal division, about the haves and have-nots, and about the nature of having and not having. Though Michael is, of course, fully responsible for his act, still one cannot but view it as a consequence of a two-sided contract of exploitation. Robin used him as much as he used her, and the ultimate power in the relationship was hers. He was hungry in her world. In rejecting him, then, she abandoned him to his hunger without notice.

There is another principal character in this story aside from the murdered girl and Michael, who has killed her: there is also the old campus security guard who finds her body, who kneels in the snow and touches her cold hair and in sorrow feels "her spirit everywhere, fog-like across the pond and the bridge, spreading and rising in silent weeping" (*FGA,* 41). Nearly the first half of the story is given to telling about the guard's past life, the jobs he has had, the way life has changed in his town. A passive, nonexcitable man, he is a townie himself, has lived all his life there and can remember as a young man seeing these wealthy girls from the college, can remember how he felt "their eyes seeing him and not seeing him. . . . He would not have been surprised if one of them had suddenly given him a command" (*FGA,* 39). The old man has never been well-off, has always had to work at menial jobs—in a shoe factory, delivering bread, and now as a campus security guard. He likes the job. He likes walking around the campus looking at the trees and knows that some people might think him lazy, but is not concerned about that, for he is content with his life, does not—like Michael—yearn for money or goods. He enjoys drinking coffee with his wife and walking in nature, and he likes the smell of fresh bread.

The old man is the counterbalance to what is askew in society, evidence of the superiority of the human heart to the elements that corrupt society—the lust for goods, drugs to soothe the pain of consciousness, the sense of unworthiness that smothers people as they see others who have what they do not.

Robin, the affluent girl, in the fog of her extreme self-involvement, has sinned against those with less than she. In her unhappiness, she has used another human being as an object; the bitter hunger for pleasure and redress against her own sense of the emptiness of her life lead her to encourage Michael with laughter when, drunk, he urinates on the carpet in her dormitory building; thus she expresses the contempt she feels for the life that is a bait and trap to hold Michael. When a counselor gets through to her, shows her that it is possible to regain control of her life, she dismisses Michael without a thought, depriving him of the comforts he has had from her that have eased the gloom of his life. He has allowed himself to be used by a person who, in turn, is nothing but an instrument to him; when the instrument no longer functions, he beats it, kicks it, like a machine. They are both party to the same crime, albeit without full cognizance, and this, again, echoes the central themes that occupy Dubus: knowing and not knowing and the meaning of these states for human individuals and human society.

The old man knows how to live and mourns the unhappiness of young people born into a world that prefers the saving of a few pennies on supermarket bread over the smell of fresh baked bread delivered to the breakfast table each morning. Delivering that bread was a function that united him to his community, a simple job worth doing that provided satisfaction worth living for. What roles will be available to the bitter young men and women to whom goods are available, but not spiritual contentment, and who seek to bury the pain of that lack in drugs and sex, in contracts of mutual destruction?

Sometimes the contract is with one's own obsessions, as in the long story "Land Where My Fathers Died," sometimes a marital one, as in "Leslie in California" and the long story "Rose." In "Land Where My Fathers Died" *(LWE)*, a high school girl who sees herself as "fat and ugly" is so obsessed with her need to diet that she gives her body to a doctor in exchange for Dexadrine to control her appetite and Seconal to control the Dexadrine and birth control pills to control the consequences of the payment exacted by the doctor for his services. Superficial notions of beauty lead to isolation and self-hatred in a society where a sixteen-year-old girl who is plump, not fat, wants "to be dead" because she feels "so fat and ugly." Her obsession to pursue a false "ideal of weight and proportion" *(LWE,* 102), and the greed of the doctor who exploits that obsession, does lead to death, although not her own. Her father finds out, confronts the doctor, and accidentally kills him, and the wrong man is accused of the murder.

Archimedes Nionakis, an idealistic young lawyer, undertakes his defense, investigates, and uncovers a trail of women patients being treated for obesity ("if they weren't fat," the doctor's nurse says, "they *thought* they were" [*LWE*, 98]), whose patronage has helped keep the doctor and his wife stocked with beautiful things, cars, the American symbols of happiness. In contrast to the false ideals, we have Nionakis, the Greek lawyer investigating the case and comparing the obsessive vanity he finds with the attitudes of his brothers, who watch with amusement as they lose their hair and whose bodies are still fit not because of an obsession with how they look but from having been naturally athletic all their lives. This brings to mind the classical Greek ideal of balance. But the Nionakis brothers, too, in their own way, are subject to superficial values of beauty and appearance. Challenged by his female amanuensis and mistress, Nionakis must admit to himself that he, too, looks at women "that way" (*LWE*, 100). And his brothers have a thriving livelihood from their beauty parlor, where women flock to be made attractive.

The Greek from whom the young lawyer takes his first name, Archimedes, claimed that if he could find one stable point, he could move the world, but Dubus's twentieth-century Greek-American seeker has turned his back on the stable life of family, for he sees no career worth pursuing that American society can offer. Nonetheless, Nionakis does pursue the cause of a mistakenly accused young man, and seeks the weight of justice to counterbalance his own irrational, inexplicable dislike of the man (*LWE*, 83). When he discovers who the real murderer is, he takes up that man's cause as well, for the problem here, like that of Oedipus' Thebes, lies not in a single wayward individual but within the society itself.

As elsewhere in Dubus's fiction, that problem is "nothing so recognizable as evil, but a sorrowful litany of flaws, of failures, of mediocre hopes, and of vanity" (*LWE*, 98) and, again, results from human isolation and lack of self-awareness. Questioning the doctor's patients, Nionakis thinks: "Their faces, I realized, were the faces of the obsessed. Always behind their eyes I could see another life being lived. . . . Perhaps they strode across the room of their consciousness graceful, svelte, stomachs flat, unwrinkled, skin taut as the soles of their feet" (*LWE,* 102).

The society that produces such a neurotic relationship to the body lacks the redeeming sense of self-irony that enables Nionakis's brothers to laugh at their baldness. Such irony is perhaps one of the most civilizing by-products of a sense of history, of one's place in the continuing process of life, of a stable relationship with the past. In such a society of isolated individuals—and the isolation is underscored by Dubus in his shifting points of view, throughout the story, from one first-person narrator to another—violence becomes matter-of-fact. As the doctor's nurse says, in answer to Nionakis's question of why the doctor kept a pistol on the premises: " 'It's just the times. . . . And you see, poor man, he was right' " (*LWE,* 96). In a society with stable interpersonal rituals, violence is less frequently evoked, is the exception instead of the rule. Where the commitment of ritual breaks down, human intercourse becomes a matter of manipulating objects, violence just another means of manipulation.

A similar lack seems to be central to the motivation in "Leslie in California," where a young wife who has moved with her husband to the other side of the country finds herself the butt of her husband's fists as, drunk, he seeks to release upon her his frustrations at being unemployed. In the morning, he apologizes, begs forgiveness, but he has already hit her on more than one occasion, and Leslie wonders if she will end up dead in her kitchen one day. As indicated by the title, this story again seems to point to the consequences of distance and disconnection: how is morality to hold up without the frame of family, society, and history to structure it? When a couple moves across the country, leaving their entire past thousands of miles behind them on the hope of a job that does not materialize, what do they have to fall back on, to give them strength against misfortune? When they break free of their entire family network, whose judgment will then inspire them to think twice about their actions? If a husband blackens his wife's eye in a place where nobody knows them, who is there to call him to account for it? In such a situation, the rituals of structured behavior break down, and as frustration rises, it grows stronger than consciousness and is answered with violence.

In "Rose" *(LWE),* one of Dubus's finest works, the marriage contract is also a deadly one, but in a much more advanced stage of development. In this story, a marriage begun in passion quickly produces more children than the couple's budget or the husband's temper can bear. The husband begins to beat the children. The wife, out of touch with the signals of her own heart, passively accepts his behavior, and even begins to lose patience with the children herself. Finally, the situation goes too far, and she is moved from her passivity. Her reaction to right the violently upset balance triggers a chain of events that ends with her killing her husband and losing custody of the children.

The theme of the story, however, runs deeper than the surface of these events and is developed via its narration by a man in the local bar (Timmy's—seen also in other of Dubus's fictions) who observes Rose drinking there night after night and elicits her story from her. The tragedy of Rose's life is her failure to understand her own strength, and that is the mystery of this story. The technique Dubus uses, through his first-person narrator, to bring out and develop Rose's story is reminiscent of Sherwood Anderson at his best, in his efforts to achieve an act of "imaginative sympathy" with another human life.

The narrator in "Rose" is a student of the human spirit (*LWE,* 181). Dubus does not give us Rose's story straightforwardly, but chooses to tell the story *of* the story, in the frame of its discovery by the narrator, who first sees Rose in the bar, is intrigued by her and by the rumors about her, and sets out to get her story, to learn about her, to "see" her life (*LWE,* 180). The story then is not only what happens to Rose, but also what the narrator discerns in what happens to Rose and, finally, what the reader can discern as witness to the witnessing. One reviewer of *The Last Worthless Evening* complained about Dubus's having placed the narrator between Rose and the reader as an unnecessary complication, which is reminiscent of a criticism launched against Sherwood Anderson's brilliant use of a narrator in "Death in the Woods." But the narrator's deviations are an essential part of this story's overall success; without the narrator's frame, the story would lose an important dimension.

In giving us the story, the narrator detours into a seemingly unrelated recollection of an incident he has witnessed as a young soldier in officer training: one of the others in the course had been identified by the instructors as weak, and they took it upon themselves to break him, as was their duty. The young man seemed not to have the physical strength to keep up with the strenuous demands placed upon the trainees. Yet one evening he walked in his sleep and was seen lifting an enormously heavy locker from an impossibly awkward angle. His weakness was not physical, but spiritual.

Similarly, Rose feared intervening when her husband mistreated their son until finally the mistreatment became so pronounced that her instinct, her spirit, took over. Suddenly, in action, she can stop the big, raging man. She saves her boy from him, leaves to bring the boy to the hospital. Her husband goes berserk then, setting fire to the apartment, but still Rose has the strength she needs to enter the burning tenement and save the other children. When the man turns his attack on her, she runs him down, kills him. Although the killing is judged to be justified homicide, her children are taken from her by the authorities.

When the narrator asks if she never tried to get the children back, her reply is that she does not deserve them. The narrator says nothing, but feels that she does deserve them, that she redeemed herself from her initial passive acceptance of their mistreatment with her action of saving the children from the burning house "on that summer night when she was touched and blessed by flames" (*LWE*, 214).

The narrator puzzles over her inability to see that her action had finally redeemed her. But he does not try to convince her for, like the sleep-walking officer trainee's strength, Rose's will not be available to her until she herself recognizes it. Rose's redemption, although unrecognized, seems to belie the undertone of pessimism here. Human life is greatness waiting to be chosen. We walk in our sleep, performing feats of great power without knowing it. If we may choose such action, we are not mere verbal shadows; we are as real as Rose running through flames to save her children from a burning tenement. That Rose awakens to her strength only in the moment of crisis and fails to understand that her response to that crisis was a choice she could continue to make constitutes the powerful enigma of this story, so closely approximating the essence of human reality, of people rather than characters, of the power and freedom of will, and of the mysteries that suppress that power and freedom.

The mystery of Rose's choice to view herself as weak and undeserving remains unanswered, as does the young officer trainee's similar choice, although in Rose's case (to see a mother abandoning herself to life without her children) it is more difficult to understand. The trainee's strength appeared while he walked in his sleep, Rose's while the emergency of her children's endangerment drove her to act, both situations in which consciousness gives way to instinctive action. The young man and Rose seem to have come to believe themselves weak and unworthy, "a belief that has hardened inside like a stone one can't dissolve" (*LWE*, 181). Now, although she has proven herself literally capable of running through flames to save her children, Rose spends her days deprived of their company, her evenings alone, drinking in a bar.

Here, again, we find a lack of self-knowledge blocking a human being from a greater level of humanity. This is Rose's tragedy, and the reader experiences her fate with pity for her and fear for himself. Rose initially failed to act against her husband because she was out of contact with the signals of her own heart. At the moment when she finally regains that contact, she is in the kitchen, washing dishes, washing glasses with decals of smiling animals on them, while her husband in the next room lifts up their little boy and heaves him against the wall, breaking his arm; then Rose at last hears her heart again and acts. But now, the immediacy past, she seems to be out of contact again, blocked by her unfounded and damning lack of belief in herself.

This powerful story moves one further level: In Rose's failure to see her own strength, the reader is witness to both the strength and the blindness and thus comes to know something of "a part of the human spirit . . . perhaps imagined, but . . . never seen or heard" before (*LWE*, 181). If Rose's redemption from her misbelief in herself lasts only one night, the insight the reader gains as witness is far more durable. It is perhaps in the privilege of seeing another's blindness that one becomes most intimate with the mechanisms of blindness in oneself.

A literal blindness of the main character in "His Lover" *(FGA)* seems to replicate a blindness of his soul as well, a moral blindness. Leo Moissant, who lost his vision the year before, lives in a trailer home where he has allowed some young people passing through to park their van for a few days. One of the girls, Linda, visits him that evening, cooks for him, and initiates an intimate relationship. When she begins to touch him, when he realizes that she will make love to him, he thinks to ask her why, but does not. He only accepts her touch, knows her only through her touch, her kindness to him. Each night, after they make love, she leaves his bed for a time, and he hears their van driving off, but she returns again later, and he asks nothing about this. Afterwards, when she is arrested and the police question Moissant, he says that he didn't ask where she went because it didn't matter (*FGA,* 31). But the girl and her friends have been plundering summer houses, and she has brutally murdered a man and woman. Linda is indifferent to what she has done. She enjoyed the killing and talking about it, but feels there was nothing "personal" in it (*FGA,* 31).

We distance ourselves from such attitudes and actions by calling them psychopathic, other than human, yet perhaps an even stranger element in this story is Leo's apparent indifference to what he learns about Linda. He asks the police whether she was pretty, and that seems more interesting to him than the terrible details of what she has done. Ironically, the prettiness is something he cannot appreciate, for he has known her only through the other senses remaining to him, primarily through her and his touch, when he smoothed his hands over her body as over "a sand figure" (*FGA,* 35). In fact, the story includes only one visual image: Linda's description to Leo of what his blind eyes look like—"blue marbles under milk" (*FGA,* 32), a striking, interesting image. The eyes are described as lifeless objects, glass, just as Linda's body beneath Leo's hands is likened to a figure of sand on the beach. Leo's sensation of touch is insular. He receives sensation rather than giving it, is blind to that which lies beyond the perimeters of his own sensations. More important, he is indifferent to it.

We are told that "he had outlived everyone he cared about and now he had outlived his eyes too. There was nothing they [the young people in the van] could take from him" (*FGA,* 32). Perhaps the irony of this is that neither does Leo have anything to give. When the girl knocks on his door that first night, he fears that she has come to annoy him with requests to borrow things, to invade his privacy (*FGA,* 32). In fact, *he* only takes from *her*: attention, sensation, the meals she buys and cooks for him, her company in his bed. She has hung a hammock for him "out of view of the road" (*FGA,* 32). Leo, in his blindness, cannot know if others see him in his hammock; neither, except for the girl's description of his eyes, is the reader privileged to see anything that Leo cannot see, for we read his world through his other sense perceptions. What we *can* see, however, are the implications of his greater blindness, the human blindness that leaves him indifferent to anything about the girl beyond her touch on his body, the moral blindness that seems to leave him unmoved by the news that she is a murderer.

The story closes with the juxtaposition of two paragraphs, one describing in detail her cold-blooded killing of the couple, followed by one describing Leo as he falls asleep in the sun, recalling her hands on his body. The two paragraphs lie side by side, fragments, with no attempt to reconcile them, much as Leo and Linda have lain side by side in his bed, physically close, spiritually distant.

Does Leo's blindness suggest our own moral blindness to that which is invisible in the objects and people we use in our daily lives? Certainly, Leo seems not to be moved by what he learns of the girl's other life, the murderous nature which lay beyond the boundaries of his blindness to all but the pleasure of her touch on his body.

"His Lover" and "The Doctor" are two of Dubus's most cryptic stories, layered with quiet suggestion of ultimately not quite accessible meaning. The violence that occurs in "The Doctor" is a natural violence of sorts, although precisely what it entails is difficult to grasp. Once again, however, the failure to see something seems to play an essential part in the story.

The story begins with a description of the thawing of winter, melted snow, sunlight, the wakening of activity. The doctor, an obstetrician who lives in a house in the woods, takes a run along the local road, and we experience his perceptions of the houses and people along the way, most of them out cleaning the dirt of winter from their lawns. He passes some children playing by the brook, crosses the bridge, runs a mile or more up the road. On his way back, he finds that one of the children is trapped beneath a slab that has fallen from the bridge, pinning the boy underwater. Trained to deal with vital emergencies, the doctor quickly determines that he cannot lift the slab, runs to the nearest house and orders the woman there to call the fire department, returns and tries again, in vain, to lift the slab. He puts his hands beneath the surface of the water to feel the boy's body there, the hands clawing at the water as at caved-in snow, pressing futilely against the slab. The doctor is devastated by his failure. When he awakes next morning, he remembers something, goes outside to the house from which he had sought aid and sees a garden hose hanging beside the door. He returns to his own home, where the hose has been hanging attached to the outdoor faucet all winter, and cuts a length of it off. He pinches his nostrils shut and demonstrates to himself that he can draw air through the hose. Then he lays the hose segment in the trunk of his car beside the snow shovel he has carried there all winter.

The suggestion seems to be that had he noticed the hose beside the door and been quick enough to think, he might have saved the boy's life with it. But we must interpret this meaning from his actions. Could he, in fact, have saved the boy, whose lungs no doubt already had water in them? Or is his action merely a gesture against the unlikely possibility of future, similar emergencies? The doctor is haunted by his failure to save the boy, burdened with an excess of responsibility which contrasts with Leo Moussin in "His Lover," and to this extent, the two stories are companion pieces of a sort.

"The Doctor" contains an underlying stream of thematic images of snow, ice, water: the thawing with which the story begins, the brook itself, freed of the suspension of ice, the boy clawing at water as though at "caved-in snow," the garden hose (an instrument used to control water), the snow shovel (an instrument used to control snow). It seems a matter of speculation as to the ultimate meaning of these details and their precise significance for the doctor's and child's relationship to the natural forces brought into play by the turn of seasons and which unite man and boy in an agonized moment of helplessness, the obstetrician's failure to deliver the boy from the water. The image of the faceless boy beneath the water, clawing to free himself, reaches deep into the unconscious, but its ultimate significance is difficult to specify. Rather, the image clings, haunts the reader as surely as it has affixed itself to the doctor's heart.

The significance of the details in Dubus's other powerful story of natural violence, "Blessings," is less ambiguous, while the human, moral element of engagement and responsibility is equally essential in both stories—again, precisely that element which speaks via its absence from "His Lover."

In "Blessings," a family on vacation experiences an event that curses and blesses them with an intimate revelation of "the insouciant speed of nature and her remorseless killing" (*Delta*, 7). The story's central character, Rusty, and her family are forced by an accident into an experience in which Western industrialized man rarely finds himself any longer: that of prey, of victim in nature.

The story opens on the first anniversary of the day the family—Rusty, her husband, daughter, and son—survived a boating accident in shark-infested water. The captain and mate of the pleasure craft were not so lucky; both were killed by sharks. The blood of the first victim attracted other sharks, and for nearly an hour the family floated in life jackets and life preservers, kicking the noses of sharks to fend them off, calling to one another to be sure none has missed a kick and gone the way of the first mate. Finally, after forty-seven minutes, they are rescued by a Coast Guard helicopter, but the young captain loses an arm to a shark as he helps the others up the rope ladder, selecting them unconsciously in order of biological preference: first the young girl and man who still could reproduce, then the middle-aged mother and finally the middle-aged father whose biological importance have waned. Despite efforts to save him, the young captain bleeds to death.

The story is set in the frame of Rusty's waking very early on the first anniversary of their survival. She is still unsettled by her memories of the experience, cannot sleep, rises, and takes a pill, wanders out into the garden as she waits for the pill to take affect, thinking about how, when the boat began to sink, the captain's error had shown in his face as surely as a cod's face was resigned to a death due to its own miscalculation (*Delta*, 15). In her life, Rusty has fished and hunted small game and felt the pleasure, "the sacredness and sadness" of killing, like something "old as the earth and the first breath of plants" (*Delta*, 13), had seen the way the eye of the bluefish glared at her from the bottom of the boat, as if to say, "I'm going to bite off your finger you bitch" (*Delta*, 14). And now she has seen the eyes of the sharks going for her family, for her daughter's beautiful young legs, and the captain's careless maintenance had put them into that situation as surely as the cod's carelessness had him go for the bait with the hook in it.

Now she has experienced being prey, and a year later it still troubles her sleep. As she sits outside their summer home waiting for the pill to work, she watches a doe and buck cautiously leave the safety of the woods to drink from the pond. Then, sleepy at last, she staggers, drugged, back to bed. As she drifts off, her husband wakes and comforts her; she tells him it was the worst day their family had ever known, but the best, too, and they share this understanding before she sleeps—an intimate understanding of the natural violence which civilization has striven to distance itself from, a terrifying violence, but one with sacred meaning, a part of the net of all nature, in contrast to the disconnected, meaningless violence fostered by the unnatural conditions and vain, materialistic obsessions of contemporary American society.

By contrast, Mitchell in "The Curse" (*Playboy,* January 1988) is cursed by his failure to act, even against insurmountable odds, to save a young girl from being raped by a gang of young men in the tavern where he tends bar. The curse, the girl's curse, enters his body like rape and "he wished he were alone so he could kneel to receive it" (180). This is the closing image of the story, and the suggestion seems to be that there is something religious about accepting guilt for our failure to fight with all our strength against recognizable evil. Mitchell's family and friends, even the police, try to reassure him that there was nothing he could do, that his choice of inaction was wise (again Dubus's stand against pragmatism), that he would have ended up in the hospital. But next day at work, he still can sense the spirit of her agony on the tavern floor and its power to curse him. Mitchell is cursed because he chose safety and personal survival over moral action.

Rusty and her family are blessed because they have survived, but they are also blessed by the experience itself, by the glimpse it has given them of a nature from which we have become so distant. And to call sacred this ultimate vision of the ultimate existential truth of tooth and artery can only be the ultimate statement of belief in the rightness of life and of nature. The awareness of death keeps us from sleep; the acceptance of death as a sacred part of life places us back into the harmonious scheme of existence.

"The Blackberry Patch" also deals with a family brought into intimate acquaintanceship with violence, in this case the murder of their eleven-year-old girl, who has been dragged into a labyrinthine thicket of blackberry bushes, sexually abused, and killed.[5] There is a movement in the town to cut down the thicket, but to the girl's father, the story's main character, the action seems a futile gesture. The blackberry patch itself seems a symbol of an element in nature, the dark twisted side of human nature, impossible to eliminate, as futile to try to combat head-on as Ahab's war of vengeance against the leviathan. A professor of world literature, he sees man in contemporary society "like Patroklos— stripped of armor and left helpless on the battlefield; we are all stripped and helpless" (*SWS*, 113). Finally, though, in solidarity with his wife, he joins the group cutting down the thicket and is ultimately released from thought and resistance by the exertion of the ceremony, despite the helplessness against its cause, as he "expended himself in the sweat and heat and the futile arc of the blade" (*SWS*, 115). Evil here has been made into a symbol, the action against it mere ritual, as opposed to Mitchell's concrete meeting with evil in "The Curse" and his pragmatic resistance to action.

In "Dressed Like Summer Leaves" *(LWE)*, another child is visited by violence, although not without some measure of invitation for the visit.The irony of the story's title becomes apparent within the first page as young Mickey Dolan, wearing play clothes in camouflage pattern with a military web belt, is snatched off the street into a bar by a Vietnam veteran who perceives him as "Charley." The reader, too, is snatched from the idyllic suggestion of the title into an immediate world of violence and fear. Duffy, the Marine who grabs the boy, is in a rage against Fletcher, a pilot who was never down on the earth in Nam, never smelled a napalmed child. He buys the boy snacks while he holds him captive, an illustration of the enemy, debating the ugly details of war in his obsessed rage, and the reader and others in the bar wonder uneasily what he has in mind to do with young "Charley." As his rage culminates, he tears the shirt off the boy and flings him to the wall. He and Fletcher come to blows, and the boy crawls off and goes home, bare-chested. "He would never wear the trousers again either. He wished that they had been torn, too, wished he could walk home that way, like a tattered soldier" *(LWE,* 77).

On one level, we have a powerful story about the violence to which children are subject in the world, the sudden springing of a trap set by the historical event of which they are utterly innocent. Any parent of small children can only read this story with a terrible anxiety about what might happen to the boy.

But there is also an inherent irony in this. Nothing very much does happen to Mickey Dolan, at least physically. His shirt is torn, he is flung to the wall, but in comparison to the subject of Duffy's rage—the smell of napalmed children which has poisoned his spirit—this is literally *nothing*.

Looking more closely at the three views of war composing the story, we begin to see an exposition of our own inexcusable innocence about what actually happened in Vietnam. We have Fletcher, who saw the war from the sky, a position of detachment, compared to Duffy, whose feet were on the ground, who was in hand-to-hand combat, who smelt the death, the flesh burnt by napalm thrown from the sky. And we have Mickey, whose father is a landscaper (suggesting an ironic contrast to what America did to the Vietnamese countryside) and was never at war. Apparently Mickey's father is distant enough from the so-recently completed war that he allows his boy to play soldier, is not repelled by the sight of the camouflage clothes on the boy who, in a decade or so, might be subject to conscription in another, equally horrible war. The boy himself is innocent until seized by Duffy's hands and rage, and Duffy's grasp upon him is a bit like the ancient mariner's upon the wedding guest. Why does Duffy stop the boy? He is in a rage to make Fletcher understand that as a pilot he does not know what happened in the war, for he had seen it from the air, where planes had cast fire down upon a country far below.

The American people were even further removed than that, rather like a child in innocence until the beast created by our involvement in that war returns to confront us, to tear off our garb of innocence and force us to know the evil that took place there, to tell us how it smelled. Of course, many Americans protested actively against the war, made it their business to know what was happening, publicized photographs of the burnt children. But Mickey is from another generation. To him, and apparently to his father as well, that war, those burnt children are so far away in time that he can casually dress in combat fashion without evoking memories of that tragedy—were it not for Duffy. Thus, the story brings the rage and the outrage forward to the next generation so that it, too, might know the horror of what the nation entered upon in the innocence of democratic ideals and domino theories, dressed like summer leaves until the firebombs began to strip and burn the foliage.

American violence, however, is directed not only at distant lands and foreign races. Although he has spent most of his adult life in New England, Dubus was born in the South, in Louisiana, where he was raised in preintegration times. A book reviewer once characterized him as a southern writer who almost never writes about the South, and one would be hard-pressed to find any concrete regional southern influence in his work. One essay has been written (see the bibliography) attempting to identify the Louisiana connection in Dubus's work, but the connections are slight at best, without real regional or sociological significance. In "The Pitcher" *(FGA)*, we do find a bit of Louisiana Cajun lore, but generally the southern connections indicate little beyond the type of more-or-less arbitrary connection of place that perhaps any writer of realistic fiction might employ, a correspondence between places described in a story and real places in the author's past. Little of significance can be found in this aspect of Dubus's writing.

In three of his stories, however, he has dealt directly with the experience of racism in the South and the racial violence perpetrated against blacks in the United States—one story set prior to integration ("In My Life," *SF*), one prior to and immediately after integration ("Sorrowful Mysteries," *TNSB*), and one with a slightly longer postintegration perspective ("Deaths at Sea," *LWE*).

"In My Life" unfolds via the point of view of a young white woman who has been raped by a black man; the story is set on the day that he is to be executed in the electric chair, two years after his crime against her. The implication is that she is violated by society's unbalanced avenging of the crime against her by a man who had never committed any other crime and who would not have been executed had he been white, and certainly not had the woman he raped been black. Thus, she is a victim not only of the initial crime, but of the "justice" meant to redress it, just as American society suffers both ways as the result of its exploitation and abuse of the black race.

In "Sorrowful Mysteries," the viewpoint is that of Gerry Fontenot, a young Louisiana man in conflict with the local spirit of racism. The story is a succession of present-tense scenes from

Gerry's life in which he witnesses and slowly assembles a picture of the black people in his community—the woman who does their laundry, black Leonard who cuts their lawn and is given a lunch to eat outside the back door with a plate and cup and utensils no one else in the family will use, the segregated movie house, the slum where the blacks live with its terrible smell like that of a garbage can of rotten food in the sun.

Gerry, when playing baseball with a black kid one day, likes him and gives him the first-baseman's glove he has earned money to buy for himself because the black kid is clearly a much better first baseman. Afterward, he watches the black kid pedal off on his bike and presumably never sees him again. Gerry tries to deny himself the pleasure of self-congratulation for his kindness.

A year later a black man is executed for raping a white woman (this event appears in all three of Dubus's race stories), a punishment far exceeding usual practice, and Gerry witnesses the anguish of some of the people around him, the sneering pleasure of others. A few years later, integration comes, and some white men murder a northern black named Emmett Till (another story based on a real incident) for whistling at a white woman. They beat him and tie him by a strand of barbed wire to a baling machine, and drop him in the bayou. By now, Gerry is in college. In a bar, when a drunken white man laughs and applauds the murder, Gerry puts a knife to his throat and comes within inches of killing him. The men who murdered Till are found not guilty. On the night of the verdict, Gerry and his girlfriend go out driving beyond the town limits through the countryside. They drive all night, and by dawn, as they are reentering their town, Gerry stares into it "with burning eyes" (*TNSB,* 136).

This is a simply and directly told story about the sad fact that many Americans of goodwill learned to hate their towns and neighbors during the period of desegregation when, out of ignorance, so much hatred was spewed forth, when the hope of compassion and change met a wall of fearful hatred, when previously respectable neighbors revealed sudden depths of unimagined primitive racial hatred and murderous loathing for other human beings because of the color of their skin. Historical events make it tempting to call this a southern phenomenon, but it was and is by no means restricted to the southern states. Rather, it was and is an American phenomenon, a self-perpetuating tangle of hatred, poverty, and violence caused by the lack of awareness that is so central to Dubus's themes.

We meet Gerry Fontenot again five or six fictional years later, in 1961, as the main character of "Deaths at Sea" *(LWE)*. He is now a lieutenant junior grade in the navy and draws as his cabin mate on a Pacific tour a black officer. The Negro, Willie, senses Gerry's guilt: "like a man who has seen a lynching and tried to stop it and got beat up and didn't get killed only because he was white and they already had a negro to hang" *(LWE, 5)*. But this perception is read into Willie by Gerry, for the story is told in epistolary form, a series of letters written by Gerry to his wife, Camille, beginning on 2 July 1961 "At Sea" and ending two months later "At Anchor" in Okinawa. During this time, we follow Gerry's sharing of his feelings with his wife about the experience of living with a black man. By the closeness of this Negro body to his, Gerry feels that redemption is at hand for him *(LWE, 6)*.

What Dubus does in this story is gently, little by little, like a surgeon, reopen the wounds of sores prematurely healed during the sixties, recalling the unhappy experience of racial hatred forced up to the surface by desegregation and the Supreme Court decisions on civil rights.

Gerry watches Willie at an officers' party control himself as he is belittled and condescended to by a white southern "liberal" lieutenant commander who calls him "nigrah." Afterwards, Willie tells Gerry with horror and shame how he knows that one day he will have to tell his little boy that he is a "nigger," will have to tell him before he finds it out for himself. Gerry sees in Willie's face "the dignity of a man, sorrowful yet without self-pity, who has endured a defeat that will be a part of him, in his heart, until he dies" *(LWE, 38)*.

But this is not the end of the story. The story continues through Gerry's log of letters to his wife, describing a remarkable series of scenes with a natural, realistic ease that develops the context of steadily rising, though nonspecific tension. In one letter, Gerry recounts an eerily evocative scene of sea-snakes *(LWE, 40)*, in another the tension on watch of a teamwork action to gather up a live AAC round which has been dropped on deck and might detonate, the strain of personal danger, the quiet courageous cooperation to prevent a possible tragedy. In yet another letter, he speaks of his sense, on watch at night, of closeness "to the love that saints feel for God, a sad and joyful longing" as he stands alone looking up at the sky out on the ocean (*LWE,* 42).

But his religious reverie and his sense of the unity of courage of men with a common purpose are interrupted with an order to arrest a Negro sailor on his way back to the ship from liberty. The black sailor had just been in a fight on the dock and had fallen into the water with a white sailor whose body has not surfaced. Gerry arrests the black sailor and takes his story which is simply that, on the crowded pier waiting to be ferried back to ship, a white southern boy called him "nigger" (*LWE,* 42–43). They came to blows and fell in the water, and the white didn't come up again. Andrew Taylor was the white's name, an eighteen-year-old from Mississippi. Gerry muses that the source of the word *nigger* "is greed for money or hatred or arrogance or some need to have inferiors" (*LWE,* 54) and that it becomes a habit of ignorance, of dimmed consciousness, of unexamined modes of behavior. He returns from watch to go to bed in the room where Willie sleeps, considering whether to wake him and deciding not to, to let him sleep until the alarm goes off.

The movement of the story is a quiet, natural one which skillfully bears sorrowful witness to the tragedy of racial hatred, the power of a word of disdain to frustrate the desire for a life based on reason and balance, on the kind of teamwork that can save the ship on which humanity finds itself, on the yearning for universal truth, the sad and joyful longing of the saints for God. All that desire for the good against a single word of spite: *nigger.* A word based on greed and ignorance.

What, then, is left for Gerry to do for his friend? Nothing more than to spare him for a few hours more the bad news that it still goes on, that all the hope of new legislation, Supreme Court decisions, constitutional amendments, of black and white people together putting their lives on the line, has not yet created a society in which that word of greed and ignorance has lost its power to kill. Society is still at sea.

Gerry's extraordinary personal determination to transcend the barriers separating him from fellow human beings cannot stop the stupidity and violence of those unable to see beyond the color of skin. A society faced by these problems seems to need nothing less than a desire for love of a quality akin to what the saints feel for God—a sad and joyful longing that can help bridge the gap between men—that dangerous area of separation where violence dwells.

Marriage and Divorce,
Hunger and Love*

> To love one must almost live like a saint. By that I mean
> the focus, the commitment, the control of self that a saint
> must have. . . . Love doesn't fail us. We fail it. We are
> defeated by our pain.

> —Andre Dubus

In an age obsessed by sexuality, the complex reality which we
lump under the word *love* seems largely to have been relegated
by contemporary culture to soap opera, popular song lyrics, and
growth psychology. Much of the fiction of human relationships—
Roth, Fowles, even Cheever and Updike—seems to focus more
on the physical and passionate hungers concerned with the individual's relation to himself and his own personal survival and
freedom than with the further reaches of communion embodied
in the concept of love. Perhaps this is due to despair of finding
a grasp of the concept at once functional and profound, perhaps
to fear of venturing from the outposts of cynicism to which
contemporary Western man has been delivered, perhaps to the
absence of an objective spiritual frame of reference capable of
housing it. Dubus doffs the armor of cynicism for an examination
of the vulnerable human spirit.

In the fiction of Andre Dubus, love is treated in a direct,
unashamed way, devoid of cynicism or dark laughter. It is as
natural and sustaining an element as air or water. Without it, the
spirit shrivels, demons of madness are unleashed ("Going Under"),
priests lose contact with their faith ("Adultery"), mothers and
fathers lose contact with one another ("Separate Flights," "Molly"),
with their children ("Rose"), and with themselves ("Rose").

---

* A portion of this chapter originally appeared in "The Progress from Hunger to
Love: Three Novellas by Andre Dubus," *Hollins Critic* 24 (February 1987):1–9.

With love, Dubus's characters know pain, but also come to understand both the distance from and closeness to the beloved and to experience sacramental moments of communion, again that "sad and joyful longing of love the saints feel for God" ("Deaths at Sea"). Yet even love, even a love of pure motive, has consequences and effects that are ambiguous, that exact a price of the purity at the core of the individual human heart.

Thus, the father who covers up his daughter's hit-and-run crime ("A Father's Story") must admit to himself, "I love her more than I love truth" (*TNSB,* 180), and it is a hard moment for him—one whose consequences touch the remainder of his life.

In a *New Yorker* review of *Voices from the Moon,* John Updike suggests that one of the theological implications of the book is that "in seeking relief from solitude we sin, and fall inevitably into pain." Thus, "with the distinct sense of loss," Updike continues, we see the Christly young Richie turn toward a human comforter at the end of the novel.[6] Perhaps seeking relief from solitude does inevitably lead to pain, but I believe that Dubus is rooting for his characters not to fear that pain. On the contrary, the Christianity in his fiction *is* existential, and seeks to embrace both human existence and God. At its height, this embrace is simultaneous, as when Richie, holding Melissa's hand, sees the eyes of God in the stars above him, where spirit and matter unite in completion.

Pain awaits the movement from solitude, yes, but so does love, which exists only in community. It is not the urge for sexual fulfillment that leads Joe Ritchie from the priesthood in "Adultery," but loneliness, the need to involve himself in the "series of gestures with escalating and enduring commitments" (*AOC,* 169) that is his definition of love. He is dying of cancer, and he seeks to share the end of his life with someone; by the force of his desire to experience love's involvement, he helps redeem Edith from the cynicism through which Hank has debased their marriage. The adultery of the title is not the adultery of Edith and the priest so much as the adulteration by cynicism of the marriage of Edith and Hank who have ceased to be fit conversing mates.

In "Novelist and Believer," Flannery O'Connor says, "The artist penetrates the concrete world in order to find in its depth the

61

image of its source, the image of ultimate reality." In the same essay, she identifies a

> type of modern man who recognizes a divine being not himself, but who does not believe that this being can be known anagogically or defined dogmatically or received sacramentally. Spirit and matter are separated for him. Man wanders about, caught in a maze of guilt he can't identify, trying to reach a God he can't approach, a God powerless to approach him.[7]

This separation of spirit and matter and the need to resolve it seem a good description of what Dubus does and of what his characters often do, beginning with Harry Dugal—who does not turn from the struggle until spirit and matter meld in understanding for him—or, again, in the obverse, in "Anna" *(TNSB)* where the robbery of material goods does not lead to the spiritual satisfaction it seemed to promise, and in "At St. Croix" *(FGA)* where a man deprived of the right to fulfill his responsibility as a father is unable to negotiate the deep waters of existence, must cling fearfully to the shore. Or, again, in Luke Ripley ("A Father's Story," *TNSB*) who, by action and ritual, transcends and triumphs over the isolation of the heart on both the spiritual and physical plain.

Dubus's characters are no strangers to God, most of them, or to communion with the deity. In "Adultery," the fallen-away priest, dying of cancer and seeking to resolve his human loneliness in love of a woman, has no problem with this communion. For him, the transubstantiation is no mystery; it is simply what takes place in the leap which the heart of man takes toward the heart of God *(AOC,* 168). Like faith, love has nothing to do with the intellect *(AOC,* 168). "You didn't realy love her, you only thought you did," Jo says to Peter in "Going Under." Peter replies, "I've never understood the difference" *(SF,* 145).

This leap of faith is reflected also in the movement of the heart of one human toward another—again, keynoted in an epigraph to the novella, this time by Simone Weil: "Love is a direction and not a state of the soul."

Love does not thrive on the literal and spiritual "Separate Flights" *(SF)* of Beth and her husband in the story of that title, or on the avoidance of pain and inconvenience, as in "Miranda over the Valley" *(SF)*, where pragmatics are used to talk Miranda into an abortion she does not wish to have; the abortion causes her a spiritual wound which results in the alienation of "Going Under" *(SF)*, where she appears again, this time unable to commit herself to the love that is offered her by Peter Jackman. The result for her is emptiness and inaction, for Jackman torment by demons of isolation. Jackman ends up with a middle-aged woman, a "sad woman whom tonight he is learning to love" and as he parts her robe he tells her, "You and I. We're what's left over, after the storm" *(SF,* 145).

In Dubus's own words, many of his characters "are defeated by [their] own pain. . . . There is always some pain, there is always misunderstanding, but those who are willing to experience the pain of love will experience joy and that is always better than emptiness."

Again, his stories signal a delivery not from the world but from evil, from emptiness, from darkness, from pragmatism, from cynicism and irony which, to Dubus, "are simply costumes that allow bitter, unhappy, overly self-absorbed people to move among the human race." At the end of *Adultery,* Edith tells Hank that everyone is dying and that therefore each act is significant. Each act is one of a limited number allotted to a lifetime's movement toward creation or destruction, improvement or debasement of human community.

As the body of Dubus's work grows to reveal its greater patterns, his treatment of human love becomes even more clearly a spiritual direction away from the hunger concerned with the individual's relation to himself toward those further reaches of communion. The hunger of Dubus's characters to transcend the solitude bounded by their flesh is where their progress toward the communion of love begins. Examples of this theme can be found in every one of Dubus's nine books of fiction.

Perhaps nowhere in his work is that progress more completely rendered than in the progress of the three long stories forming the central pieces of his first three collections (later reprinted together in *We Don't Live Here Anymore*), "We Don't Live Here Anymore," "Adultery," and "Finding a Girl in America": the first about a marriage that devolves from passion to pity; the second about an act of adultery purer than the marriage it degrades; the third about abortion and responsibility. The major focus of all three is on two couples: Hank and Edith, Jack and Terry. Hank is a writer, Jack a teacher. They are friends, colleagues. They run together, drink together, and wind up sleeping with each other's wife. Both marriages were a result of unplanned, youthful pregnancies prior to the liberalization of abortion.

Although each of these long stories stands alone, the three together are a distinct entity whose central character proves to be Hank. In the third novella, Hank's consciousness offers the deepest vision of what happens to the two couples; the final vision that comes to bloom would not achieve its fullest impact without the preliminary visions presented in the first and second novella via Jack/Terry and Edith/Joe Ritchie, respectively. Hank's presence is central to all three, even where he is off-stage, but in the third, all the characters' experience culminates in his liberation from cynicism.

The first of the three pieces is told in the first-person voice of Jack Linhart, who is "surrounded by painful marriages that no one understands. But Hank understands his, and I think for him it has never been painful, the pain was Edith's" (*SF,* 13). (Hank's pain is to await another death, in the third.)

Jack is Edith's lover. She sought him out because she was hurt that Hank had cheated on her with a French exchange student. Jack feels cheated by marriage itself; his wife is a sloppy housekeeper and has a violent temper, and he no longer desires her. He regrets the passing of his youth, yearns to fall in love, get drunk, have a fight in a bar. The first optimism of his love affair with Edith has him think, "I will love them both," wife and mistress (*SF,* 16), but clearly his conscience (or as Terry puts it, "his cold, guilty face") will not permit this duplicity for long (*SF,* 58).

Interestingly, Jack is less honest with his wife, on the surface, than Hank is with his. He keeps secret his affair until he can maneuver Terry into an affair of her own, denying her suspicions until they are both in the same boat of guilt—and even then he waits a while. Hank, when confronted with Edith's direct question of whether he is having an affair with "that phoney French bitch," answers simply: *Yes* (*AOC,* 147). When she begins to question him about it and about what it means, he warns her that she had better be as tough as her questions because he intends to start answering them. Jack, on the other hand, sculpts his conversations with his wife, selecting details to avoid problems, and realizes that he has "lost all dedication to honesty" (*SF*, 31). Likewise, making love to Terry, he thinks of Edith and then immediately projects the dishonesty into her mind and suffers the resultant isolation in the midst of intimacy (*SF*, 33). Edith, too, looks at Hank and thinks of Jack and concludes to herself that now everything is a lie (*AOC*, 152–53). Jack yearns for romantic love, but disdains marriage and feels trapped. Coming home at the end of the day seems like a journey to "some nebulous goal that began as love, changed through marriage to . . . respectable survival" (*SF*, 42). A happy marriage to him seems as unlikely as "a happy tiger in a zoo" (*SF*, 43). If Jack is trapped in his marriage, Hank uses his as a place to relax from his adventures: "he moved out from it on azimuths of madness and when he was tired he came back. While Edith held to the center she had been hurt. . . . Now she had a separate life too and she came home and they sat in the kitchen with their secrets that were keeping them alive" (*SF*, 43).

At one point, Jack worries whether Hank knows about him and Edith, but experiences an insight into Hank's thoughts—that he knows and doesn't care: "Edith can't touch me and you can't either, what matters here is what matters to me" (*SF*, 23). Hank displays his cynicism as a virtue: " 'It doesn't even matter if you love [your wife],' " he tells Jack. " 'You're married. What matters is not to hate each other, and to keep peace. . . . You live with a wife, around a wife, not through her" (*SF*, 26). Jack's discontented yearning and Hank's contented cynicism seem equally an expression of hunger to satisfy the self.

Of the four adults in the first novella, Terry alone identifies the essence of the longer progress they have set out upon. Toward the end, she comes home depressed from an evening of "sordid drunken adultery" with Hank and accuses Jack of hating her. He denies it; she demands:

> "How would you know if you hate me? You don't even know me. You say, 'You are what you do.' But do you really believe that? Does that mean I'm a cook, an errand runner, a fucker, a bed maker . . . a Goddamn cleaning woman. . . . You just love someone who looks like me . . . you love the tricks . . . the fucking and spaghetti sauce." (*SF*, 60)

Only at that point does Jack come out with the truth. And what is his response to this incisive clarification of what is wrong? He says, "I love Edith" (*SF,* 60). Terry is angry, hurt, confused, but determines to be loyal to her love for Jack, to serve it with herself—ideas that we see verbalized in the second novella, where Joe Ritchie defines love as "a series of gestures of escalating and enduring commitment" (*AOC,* 169). Alone of all four characters in the first novella, Terry takes on this commitment to another person.

Finally, Jack does not leave her. He stays, out of pity. By now everything is out in the open. Jack feels awkward knowing that Hank knows, but Hank—who has completed a new book during the time Jack and his wife were having their affair—says, "I ought to dedicate my novel to you. . . . You helped get it done. It's so much easier to live with a woman who feels loved" (*SF,* 70). Again, Hank's cool distance, Jack's guilty conscience: selfish motivations from opposite poles of the ego.

The novella closes with a scene of Jack and Terry's now passionless life together—she loves, he does not—while Hank takes up with a nineteen-year-old girl, and Edith has an affair with another man. The ending seems one of rather grim acceptance; there is something pitiful in Terry's determination to win back Jack's love and something depressing in Jack's fatalistic acceptance of his life with her. Yet what is the alternative picture? Hank and Edith's impending dissolution: Hank's cynicism; Edith's desperation. The story is finished, but not yet complete.

In "Adultery" *(AOC),* the second of the three-story sequence, Hank and Edith begin not only to experience the consequences of the passions for which they have taken down the walls of inhibition, but also to learn of a wiser love: the mystery that occurs—as Edith's lover, Father Joe Ritchie, puts it—with "the leap the heart of man takes toward the heart of God" or toward the heart of another human being, "the series of gestures with escalating and enduring commitment" which is Ritchie's definition of love (*AOC,* 169).

The adultery in this book is not that of Edith's affair with the fallen-away priest, but the general adulteration of her marriage, of the love between her and Hank who have ceased to be Miltonian "fit, conversing mates." Father Ritchie does not experience his love for Edith as a sin; he only fears it might be a sin as long as she is still involved in her poisoned marriage; were she to leave Hank and marry him, the priest would feel at peace with God again.

In this story, Dubus follows the direction of Edith's spirit—her disconnection from the daily tasks of her life which she began to experience when she learned of Hank's infidelity—his *philosophy* of infidelity— and "she could no longer find his heart. . . . Watching him talk she saw his life: with his work he created his own harmony, and then he used the people he loved to relax with. Probably it was not exploitative. Probably it was the best he could do" (*FGA*, 151). Death stalked her now—as though let in by the breach opened by Hank's adulterous heart (*FGA*, 152).

Death. Both love of God and love of man or woman in Dubus's fiction are necessitated finally by the awareness of death. Without love, that awareness is unbearable, life a dimension stalked by demons. With love—with the act of love and the commitment of love—"our bodies aren't just meat . . . they become statement, too, they become spirit," as Father Ritchie expresses it (*AOC*, 168). In "the leap of the heart to God," heart to heart, a trans-substantiation takes place which lets us transcend our isolation and brings to us terms with time and mortality—the quotidian agonies with which conscious man must live.

This, finally, is what Edith learns in "Adultery." Finally she is able to release herself from Hank, from their marital charade. After she leaves Joe Ritchie at the hospital, dying of cancer, she comes home to bed; Hank reaches for her, but she resists him. He tries to insist, to override her grief with his passion, and she tells him that they are all dying—not only Joe, but Hank and herself, too, and that that is what they had lost sight of. She gets out of bed, then, and returns to the hospital to sit by Joe's bed, waiting for him to wake once more so she can tell him that she will leave Hank, for she wants him to know that their love has given her that strength.

In the last of the three-story sequence, "Finding a Girl in America" *(FGA)*, the irony at last is that whereas an unwanted pregnancy in the first novella trapped Hank into a marriage from which he sheltered his ego with cynicism, here an unwanted *abortion*, more than a decade later, visits him with pain that flays the last hide of cynicism from his spirit, leaving him in torment. This time he is alone. Edith, having reexperienced love with Joe

Ritchie, became strong enough to leave Hank, to dissolve the adulterated marriage—the point at which "Adultery" ended. Now, alone, Hank is taking up with one young girl after another, each of whom leaves him after a year or so. Deprived of the grounding of his marriage and home life, he is hurt and vulnerable. From his latest girl, Lori, he learns that the one before her, Monica, had been pregnant by him and had an abortion without letting him know. Hank is incensed; he rages, weeps, falls asleep to dream about the dead fetus being boiled to death on the beach while he lies alongside his daughter in the sunshine.

Throughout the remainder of this third novella, Hank is haunted by the dream, and his potency deserts him before the image of the dead boiled fetus on the beach. The image recurs in his brain and is suggested in the landscape: a stranded lump of kelp—viewed out the window of a restaurant where he sits enjoying the sight of his daughter nourishing herself on beefsteak—becomes a dark suggestion. Finally, Hank realizes that he is no longer capable of, no longer desires an act of copulation that is not fully motivated by the will to take full responsibility for its consequences. Here we follow Hank's progress to the ultimate comprehension which he has been equipped to reach only by Edith's having cut him loose from his cynical mooring to his home. There is an interesting parallel between Joe Ritchie in "Adultery" and Hank in "Finding a Girl in America": both hunger to expose their souls, the priest in his sermons, Hank in his writing. The priest finally recognizes his hunger for what it is, his deep loneliness focusing outward: "He realized now that beneath his sermons, even possibly at the source of them, was an abiding desire to expose his soul with all his strengths and virtues and weaknesses to another human being . . . a woman" (*AOC,* 166).

Similarly, in the third novella, Hank at one point cannot understand why a woman he is involved with does not express an interest in reading his fiction; he feels her lack of interest as a lack of interest in that which is best in him, his reality. Both these yearnings are expressions of the hungering ego seeking to transcend itself: Joe Ritchie's hunger leads him from celibacy to the love of another human being; Hank's, in the last of the novellas, also finally turns his thoughts away from himself. His hurt at the woman's indifference to that deepest part of himself inspires him to grieve for Edith for what she had suffered when she was with him: "the loneliness of not being fully known (*FGA*, 149–50). Grieving here for another's pain of loneliness, Hank has come a long way from the man of the first novella who could chuckle that he was freed to complete his novel because his best friend had abated Edith's loneliness for him, had made her feel loved. Finally, this is a Hank who has learned to suffer—and, more important, to empathize with the suffering of others—not that there is virtue in suffering, but that, as the novella's Saint-Exupéry epigraph suggests, "Sorrow is one of the vibrations that prove the fact of living," and to be indifferent to the sorrow of others is to choose the solitude from which our unimpeachable passions hunger to be free.

This Hank is tormented by an abortion and in love with a nineteen-year-old girl who is trying to learn how to live well and to avoid the promiscuity and cynicism about love she feels her sisters are developing. Hank now sees his own daughter growing up. He sees the promiscuity of the young as a drain on their possibilities, as trapping them into temporary episodes of loveless monogamy which limit their experiences of friendship with others in a way far worse than his generation had been trapped by the unwanted or perhaps merely unplanned pregnancies. He sees that Jack and Terry's marriage has outlasted Jack's restless desires and begun to thrive again, has grown to a family, and that Jack now cherishes Terry as a friend.

At the end of "Finding a Girl in America," Hank sees the end place of the egoistic desire that has characterized him through the first two novellas, and that place is death and solitude. Love without responsibility is love without communion. It ends in death and solitude. He has traversed the maze of hunger and come to its belly, a place where the freedom reached is the wrong freedom—a freedom from human company, entry to solipsism.

The freedom that these four characters began to grope toward in the first novella—primarily Jack and Hank, whose egos needed it most, but also Edith and Terry, for whom perhaps the progress is more clarification of what they already know than development—was a freedom from the self, a freedom sought in desire and passion and achieved finally, as best it can be, by recognizing the consequences of the solipsistic yearning upon one another, and themselves, a point at which the envelope of human solitude opens to the possibility of human communion.

Fathers:
The Final Dialogue

One of my favorite scenes in one of my favorite westerns, *The Magnificent Seven,* [is] where the children of the Mexican peasants tell Charles Bronson, the gunman, that their fathers are cowards, and he grabs the one who said it and spanks him and says, "Your fathers carry everyday the responsibility to feed you and your sisters and your mother, and this responsibility is like a large rock on their shoulders that bends them toward the earth. You think I am brave because I carry a gun? That kind of courage I do not have."

—Andre Dubus

The trilogy of long stories discussed in the preceding chapter makes little or no mention of parenthood. There, men and women are primarily husbands, wives, lovers, mistresses. The children exist in a shaded background, removed for the moment from the central focus, important but hushed until the grown-ups can work out their problems. Those stories of love—of the hungering spirit's progress to the higher human state of love—might be viewed as a stage of individual human progress toward the final, most godlike phase of existence: parenthood.

Parenthood is not a static condition in Dubus's fiction. Fathers grow and develop as surely as their children do, but an overview of Dubus's work indicates this growth and development to be toward life's ultimate state of responsibility, a state of wisdom and humility, of transcendence or completion of self, and commencement of the long, final dialogue to explore the individual's relation to the divine forces governing humanity.

To be a parent, particularly a father, in Dubus's world is to assume responsibility for other lives, the lives of people less strong, more vulnerable than oneself. This is a special honor of responsibility to which one must rise. This is true for both mother and father, of course, and although Dubus does portray women in

70

parenthood ("Molly," *LWE;* "Rose," *LWE;* "Separate Flights," *SF*), clearly his main focus is on the father's share of parenthood's high responsibility.

Many of his stories touch this theme. Some do so only peripherally and have been discussed in earlier chapters. In "The Shooting" *(AOC)*, a young father-to-be goes berserk and is slain by a sergeant of the guard untested by the trials of fatherhood or by any other nonprofessional responsibility. In "Killings" *(FGA)*, the father of a murdered boy avenges his son's death. In "Land Where My Fathers Died" *(LWE)*, a father murders a doctor who has sexually exploited his teenaged daughter. In "Over the Hill" *(SF)*, a father sends his son off to the service with a gruff statement of hope that the army can do what he, himself, could not: to make "something" of the boy *(SF, 80)*. In "Delivering" *(TNSB)*, a father's "weakness," weeping when his wife leaves him, inspires his son's determination to be tough and to toughen up his younger brother. The father in "The Intruder" *(Sewanee Review)* lies to his son to protect him from knowing that he has killed his sister's boyfriend. These examples are not explorations of fatherhood but background details of other explorations.

The influence of some of the fathers in Dubus's stories is negative. We see the fathers of "The Fat Girl" *(AOC)* and "The Pretty Girl" *(TNSB)* only as shadows at the corner of the stories' greater frames, overindulgent men who do their daughters little good, whose love is perhaps too sentimental to fulfill the role of parent. The father in "Molly" *(LWE)*, absorbed by himself, his work, the "freedom of selfishness," simply disappears from his daughter's life, and Mickey Dolan's father in "Dressed Like Summer Leaves" *(LWE)*, although never directly appearing in the story, provides ironic contrast to the anguished Vietnamese veteran who "abducts" Mickey for a few hours. The father in "Rose" *(LWE)* is also absent, except in violence; rather, he *seeks* absence—watching television, drinking—and becomes violent when the demands of his children violate his escape.

In another group of father stories, the fathers are seen through the more limited focus of a child—"Contrition" *(AOC)*, "An Afternoon with the Old Man" *(AOC)*, "Cadence" *(AOC)*, "Goodbye" *(TNSB)*, "The New Boy" *(TNSB)*, and "Delivering" *(FGA)*. These stories contrast interestingly with the more developed portraits of fathers in the Peter Jackman stories ("Going Under,"

71

SF; "At St. Croix," *FGA;* and "The Winter Father," *FGA*) and in the stories focused toward the highest reaches of fatherhood ("Bless Me, Father," *TNSB;* "The Captain," *TNSB;* and particularly, "A Father's Story," *TNSB*).

In the child's-eye view, fathers often appear as alien beings of a sort, distant gods whose behavior is often undecipherable, beyond reason, or brutal as in "Delivering," where Jimmy lies in his bed in the dark waiting for the sound of his father slapping his mother and then, finally, the man's weeping (*FGA*, 99). The father's love in that story, however, is clearly *there* for his boys (in contrast to the mother, who puts priority on her own desire), whereas in other stories, it is often difficult, if not impossible, to seek, as in "An Afternoon with the Old Man," where the boy's desire to hug his father is unattainable, or in "Contrition," where the son accepts his father's Old Testament–like judgment of his ten-year-old's failings.

The Peter Jackman stories turn that focus around; the father-child relationship replaces the child-father focus. These three stories ("Going Under," "At St. Croix," "The Winter Father") present a father struggling to come to terms with his fatherhood in a situation of divorce and ruptured family life.

The first two Jackman stories actually focus almost exclusively on *his* pain of separation from the children. His ex-wife moves across the country with the children, and he must fight off the demons of grief and fear that attack him when he is deprived of the possibility of fulfilling his responsibility. But in "Winter Father" *(FGA),* the parental focus begins to expand to a compass that includes not only the pain and emotion of the father for himself but also his concern for the children's emotional welfare. This is the story of a divorced father trying to cope with visitation rights throughout the first winter after the divorce. Although their marriage has been violent and unhappy, when they realize that they will divorce, they begin to think of the children and *plan* the divorce, schedule it *after* Christmas, plan Peter's time with the children. When he excises himself from his home, loads his car and drives away, his eight-year-old son begs him to stay, finally chases the car crying, *"You bum You bum You bum"* (*FGA,* 110; a detail that also appears in "Going Under," *SF,* 126). At his new apartment, Jackman limps from his car wondering "if he looked like a man who had survived an accident which had killed others" (*FGA*, 110).

The story proceeds to a presentation of the details of Jackman's adjustment from father in familia to father ex familia. The unnaturalness of his segmented, time-measured relationship to the children is emphasized by the season. The only way for them to be together is through a series of entertainments: movies, museums, aquariums, restaurants, sledding. Mostly, it is movies, and he hides in the dark each weekend with them at the local movie house. He misses the natural closeness with children that comes of living together, merely *being* together, misses the casual meetings "between children and father arriving, through separate doors, at the kitchen sink for water, the refrigerator for an orange" (*FGA*, 128).

The thread that connects their segments of time is the car. He picks them up by car, drives them where they're going that day, back to his apartment, home again, every Saturday and Sunday. "How many conversations while looking through the windshield? How many times had the doors slammed shut and they re-entered or left his life?" (*FGA*, 126). And he begins to feel they are "like three people cursed in an old myth, they would forever be thirty-three and eight and six, in this car on slick or salted roads, going from one place to another" (*FGA*, 123).

But he lives the winter through, maintaining the contact through his doubt and pain, refusing to settle for the other pain of moving far away to avoid them. And winter ends. In the warm months of summer, finally, Jackman achieves a kind of household with the children during long days on the beach where "the blanket waited for them. It was the place they wandered back to: for food, for drink, for rest, their talk as casual as between children and father meeting in the kitchen, . . . no longer confined to car or buildings to remind them why they were there" (*FGA*, 128).

The story ends with the three of them on the blanket, holding hands, dozing in the sun, having survived the literal and metaphorical first winter of the ruptured family, which on another level suggests the day in the sun of life itself, all that a man labors to build for his family amounting, in the end, to little more than a blanket on sand. But the focus has moved in much closer to the children in that story, and the concept of fatherhood in Dubus's fiction has moved through one further stage of evolution to the higher echelons of transcendence of self.

We see indications of this higher stage in "The Captain" *(TNSB)* and "Bless Me, Father" *(TNSB),* but it achieves its most complete expression in "A Father's Story" *(TNSB).* In "Bless Me, Father," a daughter away at college discovers that her father is having an affair; she writes him a letter, demanding that he stop, lecturing him about the pain this would cause her mother. The father visits her, takes her out for a meal, and patiently guides her through her righteous anger to a questioning of her own motives. He returns the letter to her and asks her to read it again and decide *who* she was concerned about when she wrote it: the wise parent gently introducing the child to a world of moral nuance, of distinction between concern for others and for oneself.

In "The Captain," an old veteran father takes leave of his son who is about to depart for Vietnam. The old captain has survived two wars and now he must know the pain of being the one who waits at home for the safe return of the warrior. On their last day together, father and son go hunting; the breakfast they share has a sacramental quality to it *(TNSB,* 115) and the separation to come—by war, by death, natural or violent—resounds in their taking up of positions on separate ridges in the woods; the son asks his father if he would like to switch positions, but the father declines, content where he is, suggesting his harmony with the approaching end of his life. Told against "the constant tone of the night's quiet" *(TNSB,* 110), this is a story of generational shift, of movement through life to oblivion. In its depiction of "each morning having to rise from [sleep] . . . so that he could resume with hope those volitive hours that would end with his grateful return to the oblivion of dreams" *(TNSB,* 109), we discern the suggestion of a man's life span, between birth and death, of the need to rise and do between the greater sleeps of birth and death before passing on the fight to the next generation. The old captain yearns to train young men *(TNSB,* 114), but his son no longer needs to be trained or reminded. Yet the father's guidance remains as an echo in the son's heart or, as in "Andromache," as an image in a home movie of the dead father teaching his son to ride a bike, the lips on the screen mouthing the words, "Keep steering, son" *(AOC,* 107).

Dubus's most thorough and evocative exploration of the parent-child theme is without doubt "A Father's Story" *(TNSB)*. This is the story of Luke Ripley who, after covering up his daughter's crime of hit-and-run manslaughter, directly confronts the moral implications of his act and, in doing so, defines the parental function as a reflection of God's fatherhood of mankind. This is a story about the demands of moral action and moral principle weighed against the even greater demands of love, parental love, specifically the love of a father for a daughter.

"I love her more than I love truth," Luke Ripley thinks—or rather *says* to God, for he has felt the eyes of God upon him from the moment he made his decision to conceal the crime, watching him as He might have watched Cain, as he himself sometimes has watched his own sons when they were boys:

> when I was able to judge, but without anger and so keep silent while they in the agony of their youth decided how they must act or found reasons, after their actions, for what they had done. Their reasons were never as good or as bad as their actions, but they needed to find them, to believe they were living by them, instead of the awful solitude of the heart. *(TNSB, 179)*

For Luke Ripley, the subordination of the feeling of that awful solitude to positive action is "the essence of love," just as religious ritual allows "those who cannot will themselves out of the secular to perform the spiritual, as dancing allows the tongue-tied man a ceremony of love" *(TNSB, 165)*.

The priest tells Luke, "Belief is believing in God; faith is believing that God believes in you" *(TNSB, 165)*. By this definition, Luke Ripley has faith. He feels God's eyes upon him as he sins, but he is not afraid. He even talks back. God, after all, is also a parent. Because Luke's love of his daughter is greater than truth, he imagines God accusing him of loving in weakness. "As You love me," Luke says and goes out to the barn to feed his horses *(TNSB, 180)*.

Luke's love is embedded in his sin. He says, "I do not feel the peace I once did: not with God, nor the earth, or anyone on it" *(TNSB, 179)*. Yet: "I have begun to prefer this state, to remember with fondness the other one as a period of peace I neither earned nor deserved" *(TNSB, 179)*.

He would do it again, he says. For his action was a movement

from that awful solitude of the heart toward the fulfillment of his
destiny as parent as well as the fulfillment of the new command
to love one another. In this movement, he learns more about the
meaning of being a parent and about being a son of God and
being a Christian. The God with whom he speaks is not Christ,
but the Father.

Every morning, Luke dedicates his actions of that day to God,
a thing he was taught to do as a child and which he has never
stopped doing. Probably most people who have learned to do this
have sooner or later abandoned the habit, and one feels surprised
to find a character with such a direct and functional relationship
to his religion in a contemporary fiction of the complexity of this
one. The point is an interesting one. If one does not dedicate
one's day and one's actions to God, who or what *does* one dedicate
them to? What stable point of moral reference is available then?
Does one dedicate the day to one's self? To one's pleasure? To
one's comfort? To one's family? Probably the last would be the
case for a great many people, whether consciously so or not. But
what moral reference point does one have when that dedication
comes into conflict with, for example, the law?

Luke Ripley is a moral man. He weighs his actions against
their consequences. He tries to live right. He knows that he is
weak, that he has failed, that he fails. But he has that grounding
of spirit which gives him the strength to do what he must and
live with it. Like Harry Dugal ("If They Knew Yvonne," *SF*), he
knows that ultimate responsibility for himself and his actions is
upon himself. Unlike Harry, who insists that the church confront
his reality, Luke makes a private peace with his God. Both
ultimately define their own spiritual essence, but always in relation
to the new commandment: that we love the human beings with
whom we share this world.

In "The Pretty Girl" *(TNSB),* Polly Comeau also turns to her
father after killing a man. In Polly's case, she shoots her ex-
husband in self-defense after he breaks into her home. He has
previously raped her and now has smashed through the glass door
into her house so her fear is understandable: she shoots him with
the pistol her father has given her for protection. But after stopping
the man with a bullet, she phones her father rather than an
ambulance, and while she waits for him to come, Raymond bleeds
to death.

By contrast, Luke Ripley's daughter's fleeing from the place where she has run a man down is an act of self-preservation. There are a dozen empty beer bottles in the car. She has drunk only a few of them, but obviously her position would be precarious in the eyes of the law. Her decision is instantaneous: she keeps driving. Polly's action is a lack of decision; she only phones her father and waits for him to come to tell her what to do.

Curiously, Luke says that he would *not* have covered up the crime for one of his sons, not because he loves them less, but because he could bear the pain of watching and knowing his sons' pain, but not his daughter's. To God, he explains, "You never had a daughter and, if you did, you could not have borne her passion" (*TNSB*, 180). It will remain for another study to explore the paternalistic implications of this story as a reflection of the paternalism of Catholicism and Christianity. Rather, I focus on the exposition of Luke's love as the inability to bear his daughter's pain, as "weakness." Again: "You love in weakness," he imagines God saying to him. "As you love me," he replies and goes out to care for his horses (*TNSB*, 180).

These are finally the two elements of parenthood in Dubus's world: the weakness to love and the strength to care. The emotional condition of, for example, Hank in "Adultery" *(AOC)* and "We Don't Live Here Anymore" *(SF)* is in direct contrast to these tenets: his spiritual hide is secure against love; he is engaged with his own hungers, unconcerned about the pain of his family, unaware of it. Thus, the evolution of the spiritual condition to fatherhood in Dubus's fiction might be seen as a growth to this "weakness," to the openness of heart that, in weighing love against principle, chooses the former, although without releasing the latter. This is the moral paradox of the contemporary Catholic portrayed by Dubus, the encompassment into a single tension of the heart of the law of the Old Testament and the love of the New. Neither can be fulfilled by an individual alone or even by an individual sharing life with another man or woman. The fulfillment of life's highest calling here comes with parenthood, with a responsibility for others which requires man to rise, like Job, to confrontation with God: the highest stage of dignity available to man, the one closest perhaps to God. The children in Dubus's fiction look up through cloudy skies at God; the fathers converse with Him. The child chooses survival over love, the father chooses love over principle. The child's concern is with his own safety and survival, the parent's with the safety and survival of others, be it his or her own offspring ("A Father's Story," "Rose"), the victim of a crime to which he is witness ("The Curse"), or the fate of a fellow human being in shark-infested waters ("Blessings"). This is the cycle of human development that Dubus's fiction portrays—a spiritual progress that rises through childish fear, through the hunger of isolation and isolation of hunger, the lures of sterile professionalism, the selfishness of freedom, moving in the direction of love and responsibility where the things and the words of the child are put away and replaced by those of a man.

Conclusions:
Toward an Overview

I've seen the whole of my fictive world through the eyes
of someone who believes the main problem in the United
States is that we have lost all spiritual values and not
replaced them with anything that is comparable.

—Andre Dubus

The vision that informs the fiction of Andre Dubus has been
remarkably consistent throughout the quarter-century of his work.
It is a complex vision portrayed via a deceptively simple, straightforward, realistic account of human characters. It is a vision of
human beings in isolation and ignorance seeking contact with one
another, seeking to transcend the limitations of self-concern in
order to achieve a higher level of humanity. The way for Dubus's
characters to find this community is awareness, knowledge of self.
Conversely, Dubus's stories also explore the opposite condition
and the way in which it undermines the soundness of contemporary
American society, with its focus on material goods, career, appearance at the expense of spiritual wholeness and union.

His short fiction covers many aspects of American life, mostly
within the lower middle class of the northeastern United States,
although touching also upon the area of his native Louisiana. As
indicated by the arrangement of this book, his subjects are childhood, identity, the military life, violence, love, and parenthood.
This variety of subjects is linked by a progress that becomes
evident by the mere act of sorting them: a progress through time
to the highest reaches of life. The variety of subjects is also united
by his central vision and theme of isolated beings seeking the
union of love and the higher community of responsibility for one
another.

From collection to collection, this echoes and develops in complexity, commencing in early key stories such as "If They Knew
Yvonne," "Separate Flights," and "We Don't Live Here Anymore"

through "Adultery," "Finding a Girl in America," "Deaths at Sea," "Land Where My Fathers Died," "Rose," and "A Father's Story" which, together with *Voices from the Moon,* are perhaps his most important works.

The chronological movement of his fiction reflects a thematic movement toward wholeness, a progress from hunger to love, from childhood to parenthood. A culmination seems to appear in "A Father's Story" and "Rose," thematic companion pieces about strength and parenthood.

"Rose" is a tragic story of rejected parenthood and self-negation. Rose's rejection of herself is pathological; yet, Dubus seems to suggest, could she only realize the power of her own strength, the unquestioning strength and response of love which gave her the courage to run through flames to save the lives of her children, what greatness of humanity might not await her? And the children she might have shaped, but whose rearing she surrenders to the hands of court-appointed strangers, what greatness of heart might thus be denied them?

By contrast, in "A Father's Story," Luke Ripley's strength is his sin, his weakness to choose love over principle, a choice among evils of the most desirable good to be salvaged from human imperfection. The accident that disturbs the peace of his isolation delivers him to a consequent lifelong tension which he embraces gladly. Rose and Luke each have taken extraordinary action in extraordinary situations to save their children, but Rose spends the rest of her life alone, seeking escape in drink, and Luke spends his in debate with the Divine.

Dubus has never abandoned the attempt to deal directly with reality through characters who might be real people and events that fulfill Goethe's two-century-old definition of the short story as being about things that might really have happened but have gone unreported. Yet realism is only a technique, and the forces it unearths, the shades it stirs to life, are marshaled to complete the insufficiency of life itself in a dimension superior or supplementary to reality.

Thus, while the blindness of Leo Moussin ("His Lover") is presented realistically, its effect is to elucidate a situation of moral isolation. Blindness, actual and metaphorical, is a recurrent indicator for lack of awareness in Dubus's fiction as surely as it was for Sophocles. It appears as a blinded act of friendship ("The

Dark Men"), as the failure to see what is within one's sight ("The Doctor"), a failure to comprehend the pain of one's mate ("Adultery," "Finding a Girl in America") or to comprehend the implications of the clothes we wear ("Dressed Like Summer Leaves") or of what we seek ("Anna," "Land Where My Fathers Died," "Molly"). And, as surely as it was for Sophocles, this blindness is an evil, an impurity at the base of our society, the failure to see the connection between individual choice and societal consequence. The solution is no simple matter of flicking the wall switch of comprehension, for what we see in the darkness might well be terrible, yet to continue in blindness is a dead end, an evil whose consequences are human misery, violence, the failure of love.

Dubus presents cryptic pictures without answers. The stories watch us like the Sphinx, pose riddles, are often as open to interpretation as sculpture. In "The Shooting," we look again and again and ask ourselves, "Didn't that sergeant shoot him needlessly?" And: Why? A question that forces us deeper again into the happening presented. In "The Dark Men," how long does it take the reader to comprehend the captain's flaw? The captain in "The Dark Men," Hank in the love trilogy, the blind man in "His Lover," "Rose": they know not what they do and, without self-awareness or until they achieve it, are incapable of fulfilling the moral responsibility which, as Faulkner put it, makes a person "a better human being than his nature wants to be."[8]

In defending his *Old Man and the Sea* from the critics, Hemingway once protested that there were no symbols in the work, that the man was just a man, the fish a fish, the sharks sharks. When considering Dubus's "realism," it is important to remember that things are *not* always merely what they appear to be. Just as nontangible elements and details such as a character's blindness can indicate a point of entry into an entire new dimension of the fiction, so too can physical objects suggest patterns of meaning in an individual story as well as in a group of stories. As William Carlos Williams put it: "No idea but in things." Or Ezra Pound: "The natural object is always the adequate symbol for some impalpable emotion . . . or sensation of the vast." Or as Allen Ginsberg stated, referring to Buddhist poetic theory, "Things are symbols of themselves."[9]

Thus, within Dubus's "A Father's Story," the automobile, on

closer inspection, suggests thematic undertones not immediately apparent—and perhaps ultimately no more open to resolution than the Sphinx. Luke Ripley "keeps horses" (*TNSB*, 162); he rides a horse to mass each morning. His daughter kills a man with her car, a fact she tells her father as he watches her, remembering "how beautiful she looked riding a sorrel" (*TNSB*, 171). In the days that follow, they try to soothe their consciences and escape what has happened riding in the woods: they "fled it on horseback" (*TNSB*, 172). After Luke has covered up her crime, he drives his daughter's car to mass in order to ram it against a tree before witnesses as part of the cover-up story (*TNSB*, 177).

These suggestions bring to mind others, enough perhaps for an entire study of the automobile in the fiction of Andre Dubus. In "The Winter Father," Peter Jackman cannot look at his car without being reminded of the separation from his children, the rupturing of his family life it has come to symbolize for him, the opening and smacking of car doors that accompany his children's coming and going from his days. In one scene, as he scrapes ice off the inside of his windshield, he realizes that it is the frozen breath of his children. Similarly, in "Goodbye," the newly married Paul Clement takes leave of his unhappily married parents by driving off in his car with his bride. In "Bless Me, Father," the father comes by car to reply to his daughter's letter. In "Rose," she kills her husband by running him down with a car. In "The Doctor," the difference in social status of two families is suggested by the juxtaposition of Buick and Ford. In "Sorrowful Mysteries," Gerry Fontenot and his girlfriend, outraged by the lack of racial justice in their town, take to the road and spend the night driving.

Similar patterns and levels of meaning might be pursued, given the recurrence of elements such as the ocean and swimming or drowning ("Waiting," "At St. Croix," "Blessings," "The Winter Father," "The Bully," "The Doctor," "Deaths at Sea"), for the change of seasons ("The Winter Father," "The Doctor"), the use of alcohol or tobacco. I mention these aspects merely as a window to a fuller understanding of the way in which Dubus's "realism" functions and can function, the way in which his more or less straightforward surfaces on closer inspection yield implications and patterns, the multiple evocations of art.

In this essay, I have not systematically examined the sophistication of Dubus's narrative strategies or the beauty of his prose, for I was more interested in concentrating on the themes and matter of his writing, in exploring the patterns suggested by his work; I have thus looked at his strategies in the individual formal contexts of each story. But I would like to conclude this study with a few words about these aspects of his fiction: the way in which his stories function, *how* his fiction means.

His narrative strategies are varied and unobtrusive, elusive even, as in "The Shooting" or "The Dark Men," and complex as in "Rose," but nearly always both highly developed and sophisticated. Rarely is a simple, direct narrative employed ("Over the Hill" and "The Blackberry Patch" are perhaps the only two examples of this); or if the strategy is direct ("The Winter Father," "A Father's Story," "Blessings"), it is generally resonant with undertones that keep the story functioning in the reader's consciousness long after.

Frequently, the "intent" of the story seems to be inseparable from its form, its form melded with its content. As examples of this, I would cite "The Fat Girl," "The Pretty Girl," and "Waiting," in which critical investigation reveals no "hidden" story, such as we find in "The Shooting" or "The Dark Men," but where the story might be said to be a symbol of itself. Thus, in these cases, critical analysis seems best calibrated for the measurement of broader narrative strokes than for precision work. At times, the narrative strategy seems a function of symbolic or metaphorical elements in the story (the blindness in "His Lover," the seasonal changes in "The Doctor," the extensive implications activated by the brilliant title of "Dressed Like Summer Leaves"), whereas in other stories, sociological elements provide deeper layers of significance to a dramatic narrative (the material and spiritual poverty of "Anna" or "Townies," superficial notions of beauty and obsession with not being fat in "Land Where My Fathers Died"), and in still others, the realism seems fully reflected in the narrative, which concerns itself directly with the complex unfolding of human intercourse among a group of people ("We Don't Live Here Anymore," "Adultery," "Finding a Girl in America," the three Peter Jackman stories).

A great many of Dubus's short fictions offer the pure pleasures of story, of deeply interesting, extraordinary human events ("Anna," "The Dark Men," "The Shooting," "The Pretty Girl," "Land

Where My Fathers Died," "A Father's Story," "Rose," to name a few), whereas others flow from the depths of everyday events in the lives of rather ordinary people (the love trilogy, the Jackman stories, the Paul Clement stories), and some of them are so cunningly constructed as to serve as models of fictional *craft*, in both senses of the word, but craft that is never extraneous, never rigged by a switch ending or glittering surprise, always organically related to the whole. Stories like "Rose," "The Shooting," and "The Dark Men" demonstrate the fact that the taking of chances in narrative strategy is by no means confined to the technical innovator or postmodernist; realism, too, can take chances which, when successful, heighten the story's final effect considerably.

The quality of a fiction writer's prose must also serve to heighten a story's function and effect, and Dubus's writing is by turn lean as a cat and lush as a summer wood. Always characterized by control and relevance, his prose is often breathtaking, giving flesh to notions that could so easily escape the pen. It brings to mind Strunk and White's comparison of the act of writing to waiting in the bush to take wing shots at fleet birds wheeling past: for example, the flicker of pain in the eyes of the marine sergeant's fiancée's mother becomes an emblem of pain in the eyes of all women ("The Misogamist"); or consider the following words from "The Pitcher": "he felt like a shadow cast by the memory and the morning's light. . . . it seemed the game already existed somewhere in the night beyond his window and was imagining him" (*FGA*, 77). The prose ripples with sharp observations edged with humor: "If he had been able to cause it instead of having it happen to him, he would be in the major leagues ("The Pitcher," *FGA*, 86); or, "He could sense the passion and collusion between them as surely as he could smell a baking ham" (*FGA*, 142).

Dubus's prose also serves as an excellent model for enlivening sentences which in less skillful hands might fall dead to the page like a stage direction. In "Killings," for example, when the father is forcing his son's killer at gunpoint to pack: "He opened the top drawer and Matt stepped closer so he could see the man's hands: underwear and socks, the socks rolled, the underwear folded and stacked. . . . Matt watched as he folded and packed those things a person accumulated and that became part of him" (*FGA*, 15). These sentences, without glitter or ornament, are so freshly and rhythmically constructed as to mirror life, to make that which they describe real, while giving that reality the greater depth of meaning found only in language—more specifically, in language skillfully employed.

At times, Dubus achieves such startling images amidst his generally unornamented prose that the reader suddenly finds himself amidst the surreality at the core of life's mystery—as, for example, in "At St. Croix," when Peter Jackman experiences his fear of the water and allows the boatman to tow him on a float over the Buck Island approach. In this somehow eerie account of a very common fear, we are constantly anchored in solid, quietly related detail which heightens the effect tremendously with its simplicity. For example, as they sail out to Buck Island: "The long boat keeling so that when it rocked his way, to starboard, he could have touched the water with his hand, and the spray smacked his face and bare shoulders and chest, and when he looked up at Jo sitting on the port bench, he could see only the sky behind her; when the boat keeled her way, he held onto his bench and the sky was gone, and he was looking past her face, down at the sea" (*FGA,* 67). Again, this is simple but powerfully evocative via the selection of the quintessential details of description as well as the rhythms and movement of a keeling boat. Another example, from "Waiting," a description of the beach at night: "Black waves broke with a white slap, then a roar" (*FGA,* 92).

Dubus's prose can also grow lush when necessary. The descriptive details of the storm in "A Father's Story"—the trees that seem about to leap from the earth; the weeds trembling as in panic; the tree limbs groaning, swaying—literally evoke every sense, create in words a tempest of Shakespearean proportion and evocation and end the raging tension of the image, following the wind out over the sea to its death in a powerful act of the imagination which leaves the characters to face the consequences of their crime in stillness (*TNSB,* 170–74).

Any number of examples could be cited of the fusion of word and image so essential to art—word and image that create pictures and sounds and smells in the mind to become a part of the reader's life, both the conscious and the unconscious, tools with which to help the reader do his part in the cooperative effort of art, to complete life's insufficiencies, to become better persons than our natures want to be.

Notes

1. Lisa Zeidner, "Surviving Life," *New York Times Book Review*, 18 November 1984, 26.

2. The "story happened while I was aboard [the *Ranger*]," Dubus has said. "The homosexual was the commander . . . and his men should have left him alone, since his men knew he was homosexual. He had been an ace in World War II and Korea, and was the commander of the *Andrew*. He committed suicide by shooting himself. But I found out years later from a friend . . . that they had kept him aboard because they were afraid that if he went ashore he would fly his plane and deliberately crash it. So I thought, now I've got the story. I'm going to let him do it" (from Patrick Samway's "Interview with Andre Dubus," in manuscript, 24; quoted with permission). Other of Dubus's stories based on true incidents include "Sorrowful Mysteries" *(TNSB)*, "After the Game" *(LWE)*, *Voices from the Moon,* and "The Curse," the first of his short stories completed after his accident in 1986. This use of real-life incidents might be viewed as a feature of his dedication to realism; actual events, which in many cases have been reported in the newspapers, are mined in the imagination to produce the spiritual completion that will make them comprehensible. Clearly, however, Dubus departs from the core incident according to the dictates of the imaginary work.

3. "The Intruder," *Sewanee Review* 71, no. 2 (April-June 1963): 268–82.

4. "Blessings," *Delta* 24 (1987): 1–20 (quote on p. 7); hereafter cited in the text as *Delta*.

5. "The Blackberry Patch," in *Southern Writing in the Sixties: Fiction,* ed. John William Corrington and Miller Williams (Baton Rouge: Louisiana State University Press, 1966), 108–15; hereafter cited in the text as *SWS*.

6. John Updike, "Ungreat Lives," *New Yorker,* 4 February 1985, 94, 97–98.

7. Flannery O'Connor, "Novelist and Believer," in *Mystery and Manners: Occasional Prose,* ed. Sally and Robert Fitzgerald. London and Boston: Faber and Faber, 1972. 159.

8. Quoted from *A Southern Reader,* ed. Ben Forkner and Patrick Samway (Atlanta, Ga.: Peachtree Press, 1986), 667–68.

9. Quotes from Williams, Pound, and Ginsberg are from Allen Ginsberg, "Poetry of Fiction" (Speech presented to the forty-eighth International Pen Congress, New York City, 16 January 1987).

Part 2

THE WRITER:
TWO INTERVIEWS WITH DUBUS

Interview, 1987

Thomas E. Kennedy*

"The artist learns empathy from pain as surely as the child learns it from a hot stove" was how Andre Dubus began an address to a group of writers and poets at Vermont College a couple of years ago—a lecture that focused on Mark Doty's poem, "Charlie Howard's Descent" [subsequently published in Doty's collection *Turtle, Swan* (Boston: Godine, 1987)], which is about the Massachusetts homosexual who drowned after being cast off a bridge by teenagers who did not believe him when he said he could not swim. Dubus, who had read the poem two evenings before, was so shaken by it that he abandoned his original lecture and spent an hour on Doty's poem, examining the way in which it had created art of the persona's pain.

Dubus's books and stories, too, are about human beings in emotional pain seeking one another—real people experiencing the agonies and pleasures of their humanity. His interest in literary theory is purely technical, and he politely pretends not to comprehend "egghead" theoretical questions about fiction. A practicing Catholic who does not believe in the authority of the Pope, who writes stories about young men who confess that they do not believe sex to be a sin to priests who assign as penance the chanting of *Alleluia!* three times, Dubus writes about faith in a God with whom man can commune—in his case, via the Eucharist: one of his characters, a fallen-away priest dying of cancer and seeking God through the love of a woman, says that the transubstantiation is no mystery; it is simply what takes place in the leap that the heart of man takes toward the heart of God.

Dubus is a burly, bearded man, an ex-Marine captain who drinks and swears like a soldier and submits without embarrassment to the rule of compassion. Chekhov is Dubus's literary hero, God and love and commitment his subjects. Postmodernism? "It's like raw oysters and fried brains; you can't call a man an asshole

* This interview originally appeared in altered form in *Delta* 24 (February 1987):21–77.

for not liking it." Dubus *likes* raw oysters and fried brains, but is not excited by the so-called new fiction. For him, fiction is about people and events.

This interview began, in a large sense, one winter evening in 1970 when I was an undergraduate at C.C.N.Y. I was thumbing through a paperback version of Martha Foley's *Best American Short Stories* which a friend had loaned me and chanced upon a story about the painful rift of body and spirit in our civilization by a writer named Andre Dubus, about whom I knew nothing. The story, "If They Knew Yvonne," affected me powerfully, lodged into my consciousness and stayed with me long after I had forgotten its title or the name of its author.

Nearly fifteen years later, in a bar in Montpelier, Vermont, I was introduced by Paul Casey to Andre Dubus. I knew he was a writer, had read a couple of his books and liked them and told him so. We got to talking and slowly, in the course of the conversation, it dawned upon me that he was the man who had written that story I had read so many years before and which still was with me. This coincidence, this realization demanded some action from me, some attempt to explore the meaning of this meeting with the past, so to speak.

So I asked him if he would be willing to let me interview him. He consented, and over the next eighteen months or so I undertook a detailed study of Dubus's many books of fiction, compiling many pages of notes, and composing some hundred and fifty questions, aimed to help me come to a better understanding of what it was about his fiction that had so affected me from my first encounter with it—in the form of a single story by an unknown writer in a borrowed paperback annual.

I sent my questions to Andre Dubus, one question per page, and over the course of the following weeks and months, received back a stack of cassette recordings, both sides, representing many hours of the author's time as he set down his thoughts about the things I had asked and more. The result, carved and shaped and supplemented liberally over the course of further meetings and conversations, is this interview.

Thomas E. Kennedy: Contemporary American fiction seems to me to harbor two basic kinds of writer and critic: those who hold that fiction is about people and events, and those who hold that it is about language and perception and imagination. Writer-philosopher William H. Gass has said, "That novels should be made out of words and merely words, is shocking really. It is as though you had discovered that your wife were made of rubber." You, on the other hand, seem to care very much, even tenderly for your characters. Frederick Busch has said that your characters "are bent beneath a weight that Andre Dubus, one feels, would bear for them if he could—their utterly plausible and undefended humanness. . . ." Do you think of your characters, in a literal sense, as people?

Andre Dubus: Yes, I think of my characters in the literal sense as people. They make me cry when they do things I wish they hadn't done. I remember having Peter Jackman, in "Going Under" *[SF]*, in the shower for three days. I was worried about him. I wrote "Adultery" *[AOC]* because Edith started getting my attention and saying, "Man you left me in a slutty mess [at the end of "We Don't Live Here Anymore"]; how about coming back and seeing how I'm doing?" Yeah, I think of the characters as people.

TEK: Do your characters dictate their own actions (as E. M. Forster said his did on the famous *Passage to India*), or are they galley slaves, as Nabokov claimed his were when asked this very question in *The Paris Review* some years ago?

AD: They dictate their own actions and, boy, sometimes I am really happy with what they do and, other times, as with Polly shooting Ray ["The Pretty Girl" in *TNSB*], I am disappointed. If Nabokov's characters are galley slaves, I might understand why; while having flu in Iowa years ago, I was reading *Lolita,* getting a hard-on, then I got well, and never remembered to pick it up again. I do not think any good writer has characters who are galley slaves. I don't like Camus's fiction, although I admire the man deeply, and his essays, but to me, his characters are always acting out his philosophy. I can't read Sartre's fiction or plays for the same reason. I prefer the essays. I think most of the act of writing is intuitive. I think the act of good writing is intuitive, but it comes from a very conscious intellect. That might be a trick answer. I always find fiction taking turns that I have not forseen, and do not understand, but I feel to be inevitable and right. When that doesn't happen, the story dies. I always stay with those turns. "Miranda over the Valley" *[SF]* is one in point. I was hurt by the turn that story took in the end. So I wrote it again, the ending, and she did the same thing, so I let her do it. In my first novel, *The Lieutenant,* I was hoping that he would give up his career and make a stand, but I put some difficulties in his way. He had to defend a boy who had been wrongly accused of homosexuality and he is ready to go all the way and risk his career and fight the captain of the ship, the admiral, but then when the boy is killed, he stops fighting, and he disappointed me utterly because I realized he would risk his career for a human being, but not for an ideal. All my stories have changed in the writing. "The Fat Girl" *[AOC]*—I had no idea that when she got pregnant she would get fat again and then understand that her husband had never really known her and decide that what he thought he loved was not her. And that she would come downstairs at the end unwrapping a candy bar to eat right in front of him and, literally, be surprised that he was still there because she has already broken free. I start with an idea: *What if this happened?* In "A Father's Story" *[TNSB],* for instance, the idea was, what is the morality of hit-and-run? Do you really have to turn yourself in to civil law? So I decided to give a father that problem. And [I] never had any idea how that would work out. I just wanted to see how he would react to it. But I do understand the stories some weeks, some months after I have written them. I understand them fully, but I always follow those intuitive turns, and when they don't come, I stop the story until the turn comes. I figure if I intellectually or consciously force something, then I am killing the story and not allowing the character to grow. Writing a story is like love for a human being—whether your child or someone else—you have to love, be dedicated, devoted, and allow them to grow. The father of one of my students at Bradford once said to me, "Love is bidding someone to live and inviting them to grow." Something like that.

TEK: Where do you place yourself in the literary tradition? From what line of writers do you see yourself descending?

AD: I guess I am a realist. It is nothing I ever think about except when I'm reading a book that is not real [laughs]. I do not like to read books that do not have characters in them. If I cannot become the character in the book I am reading, I quickly lose interest, and I've stopped reading novels because the day after the night I was reading, I find I'm not worried about the people, so I just do not go back to the book. I do not see myself descending from any line of writers because I do not clearly see a line. I am certainly vastly influenced by Chekhov and, of course, Hemingway, who is not a realist—anybody who says he is a realist does not know how to read Hemingway. But Chekhov is the one I look up to the most. I majored in literature, but I do not remember if there is a *line,* and I sort of doubt that there is one. I think it is a game teachers play so they can have a package. "In this six weeks we'll cover this line of writers," and that takes care of that, as though they are studying evolution. I don't think it's that simple.

TEK: You say you begin with an "idea" and then invent the characters and action to go with it. But Beth, Miranda, Terry, Jack Linhart, Edith, Polly Comeau, and Raymond Yarbrough all have the breath of natural life in them. I find it hard to think of them as "invented" from an intellectual idea.

AD: Well, I don't know what you mean by an "intellectual idea," but I do begin with an idea. Beth, for instance, in "Separate Flights" *[SF]:* The idea was simply, What if someone who did not have any traditional values, had outgrown them or, in her case, had lost them through erosion more than through decision, were confronted with telling her daughter what to do about sex? The idea was fed by an interview I read in *Mademoiselle* magazine back in the 60s in which a young co-ed said the problem with birth control was that if you have sex with your boyfriend that's one thing, if you go to the doctor and get a diaphragm, you're a girl who screws. That was the idea and then "Separate Flights" as an objective correlative, if I have to talk that way, I got because of the fact that some families, including my sister and her ex-husband, who was an insurance salesman, used to take separate flights in case one of them died so that the children would not be orphaned; and the whole idea of life insurance as something which prevented tragedy, prevented disaster. Life will go on. There will be an estate, there will be some grief, but nothing important will really change, according to the values of the insurance man. That bothered me, and the notion of gambling with the mysteriousness and the sheer luck or the lottery of death. "Miranda over the Valley" *[SF]* began with an idea of parents trying to talk a girl into abortion. Jack Linhart and Terry and Edith ("We Don't Live Here Anymore" *[SF]*) all started with an idea I had in the late 60s: Man at a party was drunk and pissed off and pointed at his wife and said to someone, "You can fuck her." I had some conversations with Mark Costello about what then was called open marriage (although I understand the couple who wrote the book did not mean that to be polygamy). It was our notion that people who gave away their mates were really trying to get rid of them and that's how the idea started; then Terry and Jack formed as characters. Jack was originally a bartender. Edith just formed as the story developed. Then five years later—I had no intention of writing a sequel, I began to worry about her; she began talking to me. So I told the story from her point of view, and her character developed through her action as I let her go ("Adultery" *[AOC]*). Polly Comeau ("The Pretty Girl" *[TNSB]*) came from an idea, a true story that was told to me about a woman who was being harassed by her ex-husband and things were getting so dangerous that the father sent the daughter away. She may still be hidden for all I know, and I wanted to write a novella with the pace of a thriller. It didn't work out that way. The first draft started with the rape and then I was stuck. I showed it to Peggy [Rambach, Dubus's wife], took a walk, came back. She said, "You better find out why they're married." And Yarborough ("The Pretty Girl") began by simply some notes. He's a bartender, he pumps iron, he works out: "Don't know how I feel till I hold that steel." Which is a line my son Andre got from a weightlifting gym he used to go to at the University of Texas. So they are, of course, invented from an idea, and of course I think they are also born of my imagination. Simenon said he would start a novel by going through the telephone directory, getting a name and then walking back and forth for a couple of hours and creating this character: he owns a butcher shop in Paris, his daughter is a photographer, his old wife has arthritis, he has lived an upright life. What could happen to that man to change his life? Then he comes up with an incident. He has made up the flesh of the character and then by telling the story, the soul of the character emerges and some of that soul has to come from the writer's soul, and I guess in that sense the characters are born of my imagination. But when

I write, I always follow my characters and try to understand them and wonder what in the hell they are going to do.

In *Voices from the Moon,* the idea was from the newspaper. Simple story in the *Boston Globe.* Woman in her 20s who wanted to marry a man in his 40s who was her ex-husband's father. Against the law in Massachusetts and in some other states, too, so they planned to marry outside of the state and then try to have the legislature change the law. That was the whole thing. I tried to make up the characters who went with them. I knew a little bit about each character. There was the age, what they wanted—Richie wants to be a priest, Carol is a travel agent, Brenda teaches dancing, and so forth, and then simply put them in their scenes and waited around and hoped and tried to find the right words for the emotions they were experiencing to see how they grew.

TEK: Sometimes I get the feeling your characters are victims of Frank Sinatra and Tony Bennett: In the thrall of cocktails and bluesy bar rooms and the guy or gal that got away.

AD: Yes. A lot of the characters—that's a very good reading—are victims of the songs of the 40s and 50s. I think that music had a deleterious effect on a lot of us because it made many of us believe that marriage was not a beginning of a very difficult vocation, the most difficult one that we would undertake, but that it was in fact the happy ending, and that we would all dance happily through life and that those of us who lost a woman would indeed have drinks in the bluesy bar room and sing, "Set em up, Joe, I've got a little story you ought to know . . ."

TEK: In "Adultery," Joe Ritchie's definition of love as "a series of gestures with escalating and enduring commitments" seems to be a definition of a love which so many of your characters have missed, lost, or burned out. Why does this happen?

AD: I certainly believe in a series of gestures with escalating and enduring commitments. I agree with gestures, with actions, with ritual, more than with *talk* when it comes to love. I think that so many of my characters and us, since you ask, fail to live up to this for one reason: because we are defeated by our own pain. Our characters, our idiosyncrasies, our passions. An example, "The Misogamist" *[FGA]*—Richard Yates told me with humor and with affection, with honesty, "I'm afraid this is the ugliest story I've ever read in my life." But it is a story that is dear to me. In that story, Roy Hodges, the professional Marine can do this with the Marine Corps, but cannot have this series of gestures with escalating and enduring commitments with Sheila Russel because he cannot give completely of himself and become a whole man, assuming obligations, responsibilities, wife, and family, and all that that entails. It reminds me of one of my favorite scenes in one of my favorite westerns, *The Magnificent Seven,* when the children of the Mexican peasants tell Charles Bronson, the gunman, that their fathers are cowards, and he grabs the one who said it and spanks him and says, "Your fathers are not cowards. You think I am brave because I carry a gun, but your fathers carry everyday the responsibility to feed you and your sisters and your mother, and this responsibility is like a huge rock on their shoulders that bends them toward the earth. That kind of courage I do not have."

I guess Joe Ritchie and I are set in that line—the lover must look outward toward the beloved and try not to look through his own navel or her own navel. That involves work, and work requires discipline. We have to overcome our laziness, our anxiety, our despair, sometimes the happiness that keeps us from working, and we have to be committed, to have direction. Love requires the same sort of discipline and commitment, and it is difficult because, of course, there is always some pain, misunderstanding. To love, one must almost live like a saint, as one must live like a saint to perform really well in everything else; by that I mean the focus, the commitment, the control of self that a saint must have.

TEK: Peter Jackman in "Going Under" *[SF],* like Jack Linhart in "We Don't Live Here Anymore" *[SF],* takes the word "love" so seriously; they seem to lack the ability to develop the saving crust of cynicism or irony. Are they choosing pain over emptiness? Or are they incapable of coming to terms with the essential, ultimate loneliness of life and thus continue to believe in love as permanence even though it has failed them over and over again?

AD: I think it is a decision by both to love. I think love has a lot to do with decision and that is why I use Simone Weil's quote at the beginning: "Love is not a state of the soul, but a direction." And, yes, both choose pain over emptiness because I believe, like Zorba and many people I guess, that if you want to experience joy you have to experience pain. I do not like the word "happiness" because for me, and this is only a personal definition, happiness is an absence of pain. I think those of us who are willing to experience the pain of love, and this also applies to work, will experience joy and that is always better than emptiness. I am thinking now of the last line of *The Wild Palms* in which he chooses: between grief and nothing, he will take grief. I think both Peter and Jack are incapable of coming to terms with the "essential ultimate loneliness of life" because I do not believe that either one of them, or me, believes that life is essentially and ultimately lonely. I believe there is an essential and ultimate loneliness which one experiences within love, that there are parts of the lover and beloved which can never meet. Death is one of those. As I witnessed Peggy, my wife, having our child, Cadence, I saw certainly that was a part of her that despite Lamaze, I could not reach. I remember having drinks with a sexual therapist and his wife on Long Island, and I was talking to his wife because I was attracted to her. She was not involved in his work, and he was talking to two other people at the table, and she overheard him say something about thinking of someone else while you are making love with your lover, and she turned to him and said, "Is there something wrong with that?" He said, "No, of course not," and she said, "Oh, good." I like that, and I think that is another example of an isolation within us. But Peter and Jack choose pain over emptiness and they do not believe that life is essentially lonely. They believe in the possibility of love—like the title of that wonderful essay by the Dutch theologian, Henri Nouwens, who now lives in the U.S.: "On the Desirability and Possibility of Love."

But love doesn't fail Peter and Jack; they fail it. What Henri Nouwens essentially said in his essay was that there are two forms of love: the taking and the giving form. In the taking form we use the beloved's weaknesses and we hold them behind our backs in order to hit them with those weaknesses when we ourselves need a defense. He said that ideally lovers should be like soldiers: When they eat and sleep together, they lay down their arms, their weapons, and he says that the act of physical love between a man and a woman is not symbolic, it is an acting out, a sacrament between them, so that their nakedness is not only physical but emotional, spiritual, and mental nakedness, and he says the eyes of the lover never look with scorn on the body of the beloved, and that between true lovers, the lovers say, Your sin is my sin, your evil my evil, your weakness my weakness, and the beloved always knows that he or she is loved by the lover despite anything. It is a high state, a very high human state. I don't know if many people ever achieve it, but I believe in it, and so did Peter Jackman and Jack Linhart. They are not exactly alike, these two characters. I think Jack Linhart is a little younger. I wrote that novella in 1970, and he finishes in 1980, in "Finding a Girl in America" *[FGA]*, with his marriage healed. I think that in the early novella, he was plagued by youth and responsibility, and he cannot see beyond it.

TEK: Hank, too, tells Terry he loves her in "We Don't Live Here Anymore" *[SF]*, but from his character, I think he means something quite different by the word than, say, Jackman, Linhart, Edith, Terry, or—certainly—Joe Ritchie ("Adultery" *[AOC]*).

AD: Hank *is,* in a sense, using the word "love" as a man speaking a foreign language. It is certainly not love as Terry conceives of it. He is also a manipulator. He manipulates Edith, he manipulates his friend, Jack, trying to get him to break out of his monogamy. Hank wants fun, excitement, thrills, and he wants someone to run his home—Edith. He wants his wife and child home and to be able to fuck any woman he's attracted to. What he wants is always centered on his self, his needs and, therefore, is shallow, ephemeral. What Jack wants, *I think,* is to get out of what he *has.* The dirty house, the monogamy as he approaches thirty and is surrounded by pretty women—again he married early. I think at one point in the novella, he wants to get drunk and have a fistfight and take a young girl home for the night. He wants basically an adventure. He's a young man. What Peter Jackman wants is something permanent in the face of mortality and loneliness. Jackman, I am sure you noticed, does not have a vocation. He has a job. It seems to me that people can be fulfilled by a vocation. Some can be fulfilled by love, spiritual love, religion, whether they are priests or Mother Teresa or Dorothy Day. Jackman does not have that. He has no spiritual love. He is like [Hemingway's] Jake Barnes. He has no real work that sustains him, as Hank does, and he is left then with the need that I think Hemingway himself experienced in his life with his women. A woman to satisfy for him all his spiritual yearning. Which, I think, is damned near impossible. But that's what Peter wants. What he gets is a little bit less. He gets a wounded, divorced, American woman in middle age, and he is able with Jo at the end of that story to give to her and to heal her. I still don't know whether or not what he has with Jo is what he really wants. I doubt it. All of his loneliness has to do with mortality and he wants that deep secular love which will soothe him against mortality. It is the deep secular love which Jake Barnes needed because of his lack of true faith. Maybe a lot of us want men and women not only to help us make it through the night, but to soothe us against the fact that we will end in the grave. Now what Joe Ritchie wants and does get is the spiritual love merged with physical. He wants the love which is in harmony with his love for God, for the deity, in harmony with his spiritual love, not a substitute for it, but a movement *toward* it; a commitment as total as his commitment to Christ. Through his love with Edith he can attain the holy state, the spiritual state that he desires. His trouble as a priest was not horniness, it was—as some priests have confided in me—loneliness. He was not able to live without a family and what he wanted with Edith was, of course, sex, but something deeper, something which was *not* as Jackman wanted, a person to soothe him in his imminent mortality, imminent death, but someone to merge with him in his facing of death.

TEK: Are the emotional problems of your characters caused by being in a confusing stage of social evolution where traditional marriage is breaking up faster than traditional bonding needs can evolve to the new social situation?

AD: I think you're asking me to tell you that marriage is over, jealousy over, that all those feelings I have had since childhood have changed in the latter quarter of the twentieth century. I do not believe any of this. I see sexual love between two people who marry more as a deep and abiding friendship, a tolerant and forgiving friendship which also involves sharing each other's bodies. I believe the commitment to write and the commitment to love are so much alike. A friend of mine wrote to me after he read the manuscript of "Finding a Girl in America," and he said,

"Hank has finally learned that loving is as hard and takes as much discipline and working commitment as writing does."

I believe deep in my heart that all of us from infancy on need to love and to be loved and whenever we give of ourselves we need that one person who gives it back to us. A very wise friend of mine told me a story about someone he knew who had a suicidal impulse and every day would go through a suicide ritual, and one day he finally did do it. And this friend of mine, a philosopher, said if he did not have work he loved and at least one person he loved and who loved him and with whom he could be himself, he would be with that man in his suicide ritual which he performed every day. I think it's natural. I remember years back, during the busing problem in Boston, reading the *Globe* one morning and crying at the breakfast table because a black man who stopped at a red light in his car was mobbed by a gang of whites and he said, "They hit me, they kicked me, they threw rocks at me." What broke my heart was that it came to me that all our lives it has been that "me" which does not want human beings to hit us, kick us, or throw rocks at us, and wants instead soothing and comfort, and that is certainly love, and I do not see how Edith can live with Hank not knowing whether or not he really loves her, and by that I mean what Joe Ritchie was talking about—a commitment to love. That one person whose eyes look at her and say, despite everything and despite and because of your mortality, I love you. I think loneliness is deeply connected with mortality. I think Rollo May wrote about that as well in *Love and Will,* about the effect of mortality on our passions, that perhaps we would not have any passions were we not mortal.

TEK: I keep wanting to probe the metaphor of the cancered priest in "Adultery."

AD: Tom, no matter how long and hard the winters are over there in Copenhagen, if I were you, I would not try to probe that metaphor. [Laughs]

TEK: Well, okay, then, what about in "If They Knew Yvonne" where Father Grassi quotes Saint John as saying, "I do not pray that You take them out of the world, but that you keep them from evil"?

AD: Yes, I love that quote from John. Father Grassi is telling the boy, Harry Dugal, that one must join the world rather than run from it and not avoid evil by avoiding life, but face life without committing evil.

TEK: Was there ever a priest as open as Father Grassi or a boy as determined to protect his Faith and his right to the world as young Harry?

AD: The man who helped me write that story was a wonderful man named Father Clarence Stanghor, the Chaplain at the Student Chapel at the University of Iowa when I was in the writers' workshop there. We became friends. He used to come to the house a lot and talk at night about everything, and we drank together, and I sort of talked out the theme of "Yvonne" with him. He had come to the Church late, had been raised Lutheran and after World War II became a Catholic. He was an experienced man. He told me that the book on ethical or moral theology they used, I forget the name, promoted caveat emptor and also said what Norman Mailer has been quoted as saying, and I say this with great respect for Norman Mailer's genius and individuality and bizarre and wonderful intelligence, that rape is better than masturbation because rape is a natural act. He, Father Stanghor, burned that book when he got out of the seminary. So, many nights in Iowa, I told him the view I had reached that the Christian Brothers, more so than the priests but maybe only because it was the brothers who taught us day by day, had emphasized the act of orgasm so much that they had made us solipsistic, and we had not learned about sex in the context of its involvement with human beings, what pain or what good it brings to them. So there was very definitely a man who helped me. The character of Yvonne was made up and the sister was made up so I am fond of saying that everything bad in the story was true and that anything good in the story was not true except for the priest. I went to confession to him once in Iowa, a very long face-to-face confession in the lounge of the Catholic Union, a very long and complicated confession which I will leave in his ears and no one else's, and at the end of the confession I said to him that I would like to receive absolution, and he smiled and said, "Would you like the whole thing? The stole?" And I said yes, so he put on the stole and went to his office, and I knelt and said, "Bless me, Father, for I have sinned, my last confession was whenever, and I wish to confess what I just told you over the past two hours," and he said, "For what you have learned this summer, for your penance, say *Alleluja!* three times."

Similarly, I was once involved in a seminar in which they were discussing my novella "Separate Flights," and there was a priest in attendance, and I asked him what he would have told Beth, in confession, if she confessed her intention to commit adultery, even though circumstances prevailed against her carrying it out. He said, "I would tell her in confession that her problem is one of the soul and that right now she is too depressed to be capable of sin."

TEK: Not infrequently in your stories, a person is blocked from the religion which sustains his or her spirit due to human needs which they cannot and never will be able to avoid. In "The Pretty Girl," Polly's desire for grace is blocked by a provincial view of Church law, even though she is not certain that making love is a sin.

AD: Polly is morally lazy, and it is connected with her being a pretty girl, not a woman, but having grown up pretty and with a father who loves her very much. She approached womanhood expecting something because she is American, she is white, and she is pretty. What she does not approach the grown-up world expecting is to work, to search, most of all to search, to be curious, to find, to grow, and—to quote Walter Mondale—to open doors. So she knows something is wrong with her. But she does not know exactly what. She is lukewarm. I don't see any indictment of the Church in this. Polly believes "her life is not a good one, though in a way the church had never defined." Polly is lazy, lacks imagination, and she knows she is living in first gear.

TEK: In "Separate Flights," Beth feels ashamed when she gossips, ashamed when she masturbates. When she tells an insignificant lie to her daughter, she feels more lonely. She says to her husband, "I talked about you. I couldn't have been more unfaithful." Is this part of Beth's malaise, her inability to don the saving armor of cynicism or to develop a taste for the spice of irony? Neither is she able to equip her daughter with these tools—instead she gives the girl the nakedness and vulnerability of disillusionment.

AD: Beth feels ashamed when she gossips because [laughs] I think gossip is bad. At that time in her life she is trying to look

at its various pieces to see what they form, and her social relationships with women seem to be largely based upon gossiping
about somebody. I don't think she thinks about this as a serious
evil, but rather as something less "good" than she would wish
for. The guilt she feels when she masturbates is an extension of
what she sees as her infidelity to her husband (saying derogatory
things about him to a man to whom she is attracted), which is
a symptom of the death of love she has felt for her husband;
doing it beside him while he sleeps is, to her, a dramatization of
how isolated from him she has not only become but has now
chosen to become. When she lies to her daughter, she feels more
lonely because the lie puts her further from her beloved and
increases her isolation. Compare this with what Edith learns from
her love of Joe Ritchie when he is dying and what she tells her
husband, Hank, at the end of "Adultery," that we are all dying
and that each act is significant. Each act between people who love
each other, not just man and woman, but filial love, paternal
love, fraternal love, all of it, should ideally be actions and words
which are exchanged while you're sitting on the wharf waiting for
Charon to come take you across the river Styx. Beth's shame and
guilt are just further symptoms of a central loss which is no longer
knowing why she exists. To paraphrase Chekhov in *The Three
Sisters,* if you don't know why the grass grows, why birds fly,
etc., then everything is just wild grass. I almost called that story
"Wild Grass." As for cynicism and irony, these are simply costumes that allow bitter, unhappy, overly self-absorbed people to
move among the human race. And thank god she does not try
to give these to her daughter. What she tries to give her daughter
is truth. The terrible thing is she understands she has no truth
to give. So the daughter is left with, in your phrase, "the nakedness
and vulnerability of disillusionment." She doesn't grow beyond
these frames because she stopped going to church—nothing wrong
with that in itself, but she never replaced religion, by which I
mean a deep and abiding philosophy, with any other philosophy.
Again, spiritual laziness. When the time came that she needed a
truth for her daughter, she had none. To paraphrase a Chekhov
story from which I took a quote for an epigraph for *Adultery and
Other Choices,* when you have no force outside of yourself, everything is a symptom, and nothing more.

As for gossip, for a long time, until I was thirty, I did confess gossiping about people. I thought it was bad. I finally gave in and joined the rest and I do not say that to blame the rest. I finally just started doing it. I gossip now, and I do not think it is good, but I am not sure how much it has to do with this question. I know I felt better when I did not say bad things about people. At times, of course, there are sons of bitches who deserve it.

TEK: In the powerful story "Contrition," the boy Paul seems to accept responsibility for what happens, accepts his father's severe judgment of the boy's worthlessness, and in so doing sees ". . . the narrow breadth of his soul which in ten years had learned nothing of courage and so much of lies." Your young people look up through the rain at God, do not grow passive under spiritual agony, but train the powers of their intellect to the protection and preservation of their faith. Is this a reflection of the objectively real world, or are your stories a more imaginative realm in which you create a vision of matter and spirit in juxtaposition?

AD: I have six children. I remember my childhood. I think children know a lot, and I think a child certainly can understand that his father is not a brute and that he, himself, bears some responsibility. I was very happy to read in Nadine Gordimer's new collection, *Something Out There,* "A Letter to His Son." This is Franz Kafka's father writing to him from the afterlife. Every writer should read it because it makes us understand that it is not so much fun for parents to live with a writer either. Paul's final insight in my story is an understanding of his father and himself and that he is not the best of sons for a normal father to have, and I see that as a sad, maybe even tragic moment that the son experiences when he understands what it is like to be the father of him.

TEK: At the end of "Miranda over the Valley," Miranda leaves Michaelis "lying naked in the dark." Has she left illusion behind?

AD: That ending surprised me more than most of my endings do. I wrote it over two times, hoping that she would do something different, but she didn't. I saw her as defeated. As a friend and poet, Kenneth Rosen, said, "She was defeated by reason over instinct." That her parents and Michaelis, who failed her, had defeated that "leap of the heart" she had made in giving her virginity and deciding to have the baby and deciding that she wanted Michaelis and did not want to live as Holly, her roommate, did, and he is by the way called Michaelis because Michaelis was Lady Chatterley's first lover, a selfish little prick. I was just playing around with that. The story is full of all sorts of religious symbols, too, which I stuck in for my own reasons and hoped that no reader would ever discover. But I found that she had become disillusioned and had learned nothing about love. Which is why in the later story, "Going Under," she could not make a commitment because of what happened to her at eighteen when she was ready to be *afraid*—something which Americans are terrified of. She was ready to be afraid, ready to give up safety, she was ready to give up practicality, pragmatism. I had her reading Anouilh's *Antigone* on purpose because in it, Antigone says to Creon, "I refuse to live in the world that you live in." Pragmatic. And if I had written an epigraph for that story, it would have been from another Anouilh play called *The Rehearsal,* in which a young, innocent, and good woman says, something like, *"Practical. Everytime somebody says that word, I know they are getting ready to do something bad."*

TEK; "The Fat Girl," "The Pretty Girl," "Finding a Girl in America" . . . do you use the word "girl" ironically? affectionately? historically? sociologically?

AD: "The Fat Girl" and "The Pretty Girl" are called girls because the troubles they go through occur in their girlhoods. "The Fat Girl" is taken through high school and college when she becomes a svelte woman and a wife. She is still in her heart a fat girl. People tell me I am a *big* man. I am not. I am still inside the guy who weighed 105 pounds when I got my driver's license at the age of fifteen or sixteen. "The Pretty Girl" is a woman who is suffering from having been a pretty girl. She is not a full woman yet, so that is her hangover from her girlhood, the pretty girl. "Finding a Girl in America" is simply a choice of a word for the rhythm of it. I just didn't think "Finding a Woman in America" sounded as good. I do not call women girls. It pisses them off, so it's fine with me to call them women. I notice that working women say "the girls" as men say, "I'm going out drinking with the boys." Working women say, "The girls and I are going out for a drink" But since other women consider that an insult it is fine with me to call them women.

TEK: In my opinion, you write startingly well from the point of view of a woman. I'm thinking of Edith in "Adultery," of Beth in "Separate Flights," and of Miranda in "Miranda over the Valley," to name three. To what do you attribute this ability? Is the jump from one heart to another of equal distance whether from man to man or man to woman?

AD: Nadine Gordimer, in her introduction to her selected stories, deals with this entire problem by saying that all writers are androgynous, and I believe it. I am stunned—and I am not putting you down, my friend—at how often I am asked in interviews how I can write about women, when I meet women all the time who write well about men, and I think the real answer to your question is, as you say, the jump from one heart to another is of equal distance whether from man to man or man to woman. I think that is the answer. There is something universal in all of us. Some female characteristics I would not be able to write about without asking a woman, but I've spent a lot of time asking women, and I have always been interested in women. I have always enjoyed talking to women, I love women. If you are interested in a certain type of person, and you love the type of person, it is not that difficult to become them and write about them. I think I would have a lot easier time writing about a woman than I would, for instance, about a fictional Ronald Reagan.

TEK: I wonder about the "lukewarm" epigraph to "The Pretty Girl." Who is lukewarm? Polly? Why? Because she sought shelter in a man and marriage after realizing that no more summer vacations awaited her?

AD: Polly is lukewarm. She has a lot of potential. She is maybe the only morally and intellectually lazy person I've ever written about. She's a C-student on purpose. She's lukewarm because she did have what in many cases is the bad luck to be a pretty girl in a country which honors that, and she had somewhat of a doting father. That's all she ever needed. It got her all the attention she needed. All this business about her marrying and realizing that there are no more summer vacations and joining the world of work were awakenings to her that should not have been awakenings. She should have known. I love Polly very much. My problem with her is that she has allowed the physical beauty of her face to dictate her direction and once she reaches the adult world where it is no longer a viable commodity—she is not, after all, trying to be an actress—then all her expectancy becomes precisely what she earned: C's. And her expectancies have a C-grade to them because they are shabby fulfillment. There is a time in that novella when she has the flu and is trying to remember the pleasure of childhood, when she has certain insights and realizes that there is a part of her she is not fulfilling because she's never paid attention to it. That she has this vague sense of doing something immoral although it is not something the Church defines. It's that she is not trying to fulfill herself as a human being, and I am not suggesting anything—marriage, vocation as opposed to job, anything, but I am pulling strongly for her to try to *know* herself, which she never does in the story. Which is why I think she ends up killing Ray and not knowing what to do because the poor bastard does bleed to death after she shoots him. She goes and calls her father instead of an ambulance.

TEK: In "Finding a Girl in America," Hank goes for the newer generation of women. Was his own generation too "lukewarm"? What will happen to those women?

AD: Hank goes for the new generation of women for two reasons: one, he is living in a dead milltown where his only choices of women are students, mill workers, or secretaries. Out of context, this sounds snobbish, but Hank is intellectual, and he is looking for a companion. So there is the proximity of the girls in the college. That is the first reason. The second is the divorcées of his own age—now this is not a statement about all divorcées, only his experience, which is limited, he does not live in an urban area or in a large university where he might meet graduate students, for example, or other teachers—he has only one love affair with a woman near his own age, and she is too embittered, too fragile, too hurt by her divorce and doesn't know who she is. Also, she is not interested in his work, which baffles him, not because of vanity, but because his work *is* him, and if she doesn't like his work who in the hell is she making love with? But no, she is not lukewarm. She is impassioned, but the desperation that has her searching—a fear, a long-nurtured sadness and bitterness—makes her unapproachable for him, for the kind of harmonious union he is looking for. The woman he finally does fall for is young, and the reason he loves her is that she is a good human being

107

and so far she is untouched. This has nothing to do with female liberation. She is trying to find out what she is. Her mother wants her to get good grades and go to graduate school, but Lori is one of those people—men and women both—who really don't see a vocation out there. Certainly, my twenty-four- and twenty-five-year-old sons are going through the same thing, and I think it is because we have a shabby capitalistic society which is not concerned with the fulfillment of human beings and with the welfare of human beings so much as it is with getting people to make someone think they want to buy something, getting some other people to get paid to make it, and getting some other people to get the most money for having them make it, and hiring the people to make people want it. How many jobs can you really think of out there that are worth a damn? Lori doesn't want any of them. She doesn't have the drive for a particular vocation, but what she wants to do is more important. She wants to be a good human being. She is also rebelling against some bad parts of the sexual revolution—I am certainly not against the sexual revolution—but she says to Hank, we're not gonna raise a goddamn American. She wants values, she wants love, she wants commitment.

TEK: Do you think of yourself as an American, at home in the American culture, in the daily life surrounding you, or are you alienated from it, or from aspects of it? Do you have faith in the political and social patterns of America?

AD: Yes, I am American at home in the American culture and in the daily life surrounding me. I am alienated from aspects of it, especially in the direction that American politics is going—that is, nationalizing and sanctifying greed, but calling it something else. I do not have faith in the political and social patterns of America. I see the country getting more and more greedy and I deeply believe that if the country is going to continue to be based on greed and selfishness, that it doesn't really deserve to survive, but of course the victims of this greed and selfishness deserve to survive so what do you do about that? You can't have a revolution. The government has all the guns, and besides, my scant knowledge of history tells me every time there is a revolution, the mother-fuckers who take over do the same thing. I am absolutely in favor of socialized medicine or some sort of national medical care. I don't think anyone should be afraid to get sick. I don't think the poor should have rotten teeth in their mouths. I don't think our friend's baby should have died in Maine because she couldn't afford medical care. I am in favor of people who work at a place jointly owning that place. I guess that's socialism. I like two views—Tolstoy's, if you have a culture based on Christian values where each person is trained to help the other, then you will still have murderers and rapists, but you will not *create* any. We certainly create them. And I like what Einstein said in an essay that our education is all wrong, we should not be taught to compete; we should be taught to work for the common good.

TEK: You write a lot of stories about murder and violence—"The Pretty Girl," "Killings," "The Shooting," "Townies," and in *The Times Are Never So Bad,* you use a Flannery O'Connor epigraph about how violence strips the personality to what is eternal. Is this violence a reflection of American consciousness, of your own, of both, or more of an attempt to reach that eternal vision of the human personality?

AD: I think it is mostly a reflection of American consciousness. I think if I lived in Canada or Denmark, I probably wouldn't write much violence. One of my son's girlfriends was mugged. My twenty-one-year-old daughter risked her life because a person was pointing a gun at the window of a teacher my daughter was going to visit. Someone else very close to me was raped. And I can't read the paper, even the local one, without coming across violence. I see this country as becoming a very violent country and I react to it. I do not think my own consciousness is violent. The eternal vision of the human personality: Well, Peggy read me that quote from Flannery O'Connor, and I stole it because it was wonderful for an epigraph and is probably true in some cases. I think my attitude about violence is expressed in "Killings." As in "Man's Fate," the assassin comes back from stabbing this guy, and they are all talking about the wonderful new world they will have under communism, and he says, "What about me?" And you realize the act of killing has removed him from nature and the same thing with Matt Fowler in "Killings." Once he kills a human being, he has violated nature and is forever removed from it.

TEK: In "The Pretty Girl," when Raymond rapes Polly, he

109

feels "mended," while she consequently experiences "her very life as a sin, her every action soiled by an evil she could not name." Why is this?

AD: I finally figured out why Raymond was so disturbed. He couldn't enjoy his workouts. It wasn't the past, as it is with many relationships. We ache because of what she or he did to us in the past. Ray has recovered from that. He's a strong man. He knows he can go under and lose his life for a few days, and then he knows that if he works out, he can walk into the world again and sign his name on a check and feel like he exists in the world. But she put him through so much pain that he cannot bear imagining her walking around that same moment breathing a portion of the same air he's breathing. So when he rapes her, he feels as though something in him has been returned which was taken away, something was healed. Polly, who lives in low gear, knows something is wrong with her life. Her every action is soiled by an evil she cannot name. It is simply the way she lives—like a flower, but she is not a flower. A flower lives a perfect life. She simply turns her face to the sun. She gets nourished by water. When it is cold, she wilts. She does not take control of her life and probably beneath that is a deep selfishness. She is unable to love because she has never given herself a direction.

TEK: For five and a half years, you were a captain in the Marine Corps—a warrior artist. How did that feel?

AD: If you mean by warrior some berserk blood-stained guy enjoying killing people, I never had that feeling. If you mean a professional soldier, that is what I felt like. I didn't want a war. As a young man, I wanted to live an active life and keep that apart from my artistic life. But I resigned from the corps because my father died. Only later did I realize it was my father's death that gave me the freedom to resign. My respect for him and my need for respect from him were not greatly diminished by distance and by age. I do not think I would have had the courage while he was alive to explain to him that I was leaving a good and secure and honorable, in those days, profession, and was going to take a family of one wife and four children to Iowa City for an assistantship of $2,400 a year.

TEK: In "Cadence," Paul finally is driven by the Marine Corps drill instructor to transcend a point of fatigue and finally wins the respect of the D.I. and his place amongst the "herd." His friend, Hugh Munson, however, gives up. He asks, "What's the point of doing something that makes you puke? . . . Is that smart, man?" What will happen to Munson on the outside? Will the "failure" of his manhood drive him mad, as the D.I. suggests, or will his intelligence and sound emotion make it possible for him to transcend the pattern? And how about Paul? Is he victor or victim? Does he find himself in the herd, or lose himself there?

AD: Another close friend of mine who read "Cadence" said that the real hero is Munson and the villain Paul, and I think he got the point precisely. Nobody who has ever talked to me about the story has mentioned the importance of the fact that Munson does not have a father and does have a girlfriend. He has what a man needs. He has his life, his girl, he does not need to prove to himself what Paul does. So Munson makes sense when he says "Is this smart? To run till you puke?" I think he gets along fine. I think Munson went back to New York and lived a normal life and had no problem and that Paul's failure is that he has to prove to himself that he is a man and prove it to his father, which is the reason for the flashback to the construction job (that is an actual scene from my life), and the reason also that he is more afraid of quitting, of going home to face his father, than he is of continuing the endurance of Marine Corps training. I think Munson will transcend this. Paul is both victim and victor. He finds himself a part of the herd, but he gives up his loyalty to his friend. So he chose the herd because by earning the right to be in the herd he got self-respect, but the price he paid for that was a moral one. He also ignores Munson at the end. Munson was his friend, and Paul let him down so I thought the *real* man in the story was Munson, although I did love and respect everyone in there, including Sergeant Hathaway, who is doing his job as he should do it, fulfilling his vocation.

TEK: From professional soldier to professional ballplayer: "The Pitcher" seemed to me a story not only about a baseball player, but about the artist and about the conflict between a human being's responsibility to his talent and to his family and the unknowing attempts his family will make to deter him from discovering that which is trying to imagine him. There seemed no question to me that the pitcher's gift was something like the will of God and that he must serve as vehicle of that will. Is the exercise of talent an inevitable demand of existence for those who have it? Does Billy have free will or is he possessed of his talent? Could he choose Leslie (or any other human being or cause—if he had children, for example, or *was* called to war) over his calling as a pitcher? Is the artist destined to be more alone than others, in obedience to the sources of his talent?

AD: It could be about an artist, but I think it's more about a professional. Of course, I was thinking about a writer, but only as a means of getting into the pitcher, assuming that certain writers, certain athletes, certain policemen, certain plumbers feel in a similar way about their work. Yes, no question, Billy Wells must serve as a vehicle for his talent, for the gift that he has, but I don't think the exercise of talent is an inevitable demand of existence, although it may be so for those Stendhal cited at the end of his books *The Red and the Black* and *The Charterhouse of Parma*—with his dedication to "the happy few." I don't think everybody has a talent or needs to have one. I think Billy has free will. He is possessed of his talent, but talent is cheap: he keeps that talent by discipline. Probably more have destroyed good talent than have gone on to devote their lives to it. It takes discipline and commitment. I do think that he can choose. I do not think the artist is destined to be more alone than others. I think that is romanticized bullshit. I like what Joseph Conrad says about work in *Heart of Darkness: I don't like work, no man does, but I like what is in the work.*

R. V. Cassill, when we were at Iowa, told us once there were 100 of us in the fiction workshop, and ninety of us would be sheep, ten would be goats. By goats, he meant those who would publish. Out of those ten, three or four of us would publish *a* book, a novel, a book of stories, the other six or seven would publish forever. I think most writers quit between the ages of twenty and thirty for various reasons. They are alone then unless they have exceptional parents; even if they have very loving and tolerant parents, they still know in their heart of hearts that their parents wonder about what in the fuck they are doing. Unless they live in a community of writers, like at a graduate school, they don't have friends who really understand what they are doing. They don't get published. They work, and of course don't get money for it. There is no one to set the alarm clock for. There is no one who cares whether they get there to work, no one who can threaten them with firing nor reward them with money, and you put all of that on one poor young man or woman's back, and it takes an awful lot of courage, because it comes down to that person believing in him or herself and saying I will do it. While having a job which supports me. And you may have experienced this, you know, you finally do publish in something as lovely as *Tendril* or *Ploughshares,* for example, and you call your mother or father and tell them, and they say, "What's that?" I think that is why young writers can be persuaded so easily to change things to be in the *New Yorker.* Not for the goddamn money. What's $3,000 gonna do? You can't live in Mexico on it and write. Not for long anyway. Won't change your life. I think they do it because it takes care of those blank faces when you say, Yes, I've published, and they say, 'Where?" and you say, "The *New Yorker,*" and they say, "Ooooo! You must be real!" I think that's the only lonely time. The rest of the time, we write alone, of course, but we are not really alone. We have our characters. We are no more alone than a person playing a piano or painting a picture or training a horse or training for an athletic meet. It is a fulfilling loneliness.

TEK: Technical question: In his biography of Max Perkins, A. Scott Berg reports how Perkins took seriously more than any of his authors (Hemingway, Fitzgerald, Lardner) the arrangement of stories in a collection and would generally take responsibility for doing this, arranging them after a system gauged to maintain reader interest. I would like to ask whether the arrangement of stories in your many collections are important to their reading? Is a specific relationship and, thus, meaning created by the arrangement of the stories, or would this be an imaginative act by the reader, as Wright Morris puts it?

AD: The arrangement is important to the reading, and I do take the trouble. I learned that from Richard Yates and assume that all short-story writers take the trouble. Therefore, when I buy a book of stories, I read them in order. I do arrange mine, but I don't know if they make any sense. I remember showing Mark Costello one of my tables of contents once and asking him what he thought, and he said he guessed there was some sense to it, but didn't know. The arrangement of *Adultery and Other Choices* was Godine's idea, and I agreed with it. I had no idea of what to do, and he said, why don't we put the stories of youth first. So "Graduation" and "The Fat Girl" end up there with three Paul Clement stories and another Paul Clement story appears in the military section, and that was simply the idea of putting the young peoples' stories first, then the military, and then the novella and that made sense to me. With *Finding a Girl in America,* I started with the most violent and lumped them together and then moved into a second section which was sort of a hash and that didn't really fit anywhere, but what I was trying to do was move up from violence to what I thought was the first celebrative ending I had ever written in my life. So I wanted the reader to end up with [chuckles] I don't want to say "a happy ending" [laughs], but celebrative, affirmative.

Dick Yates once told me he arranged *Eleven Kinds of Loneliness* by moving from the simplest story to the more complex. That's what I generally keep in mind. But I do not think that is precisely the way it has worked. *The Times Are Never So Bad* begins with the novella and ends with "A Father's Story" because once again I wanted the last story to be more uplifting, which is the same reason I asked Crown when they collected the four novellas, even though "The Pretty Girl" was the most recent, to put that one first because I think it is a very bleak story. It hurt me. When it ended, I was hoping that Ray and Polly would get together. Instead, she shot him and then I found out she let him goddamn bleed to death waiting for her Daddy, and so I thought that should go first in the collection and the more celebrative "Father's Story" last.

TEK: What writers have you learned most from? Who are your major influences?

AD: I learned the most when I was young from Hemingway and a lot of that was physical stuff. Stopping a sentence in midline. Stopping your work for the day when you are still going well. Exercising afterwards and trying never to think about your work when you are not actually at the desk. Hemingway inspired my romantic side when I was eighteen or nineteen. I thought it would be great to walk around with a beret and go to bullfights and shit like that. But my major influence is Anton Chekhov. I think a trace of Faulkner comes into my prose sometimes, but Chekhov is the one who really grabbed my heart and kept it. Because of how much he could get done in so little. Nobody can touch him when he goes over twenty-five pages. When he gets up to a hundred, everybody bows. Because of his enormous compassion for his characters, because of his ability to bring his characters to life and because of his own dictum he stuck to so well: you won't find me in my stories. Even in one of my favorite stories of his, called "A Dull Story" or "A Dreary Story," depending on the translation you read, in which he wrote to his editor, this story is full of ideas, and none of them is mine.

TEK: Which of your contemporaries and which of the younger generation of writers do you read and find exceptionally good?

AD: This is dangerous. I am bound to leave somebody out. there are so many. John Yount and Paula Fox, I think, are America's greatest living novelists. I think Gina Berriault is our greatest living short-story writer. I think Nadine Gordimer is internationally a great short-story writer and an equal of Gina Berriault. I like Tobias Wolff, I like Raymond Carver. I like the galleys of the first book of stories I just read by a woman named Sharon Sheehe Stark (*The Dealers Yard,* 1985; *The Wrestling Season,* 1986). I like Susan Dodd (*Old Wives' Tales,* 1984; *No Earthly Notion,* 1986). I do reread Chekhov. I like a book of stories by Nancy Huddleston Packer called *Small Moments,* published by the University of Illinois Press which published my old friend Mark Costello's *The Murphy Stories.* Contemporaries. Contemporaries. I like Thomas Williams, Mark Smith, I like Kate Chopin, though she is not a contemporary. I like Philip Caputo. Not only for nonfiction *(Rumor of War)* but his two novels. I once tried to convince Dick Yates to read Caputo's novels, and he said, "Well, I don't read novels by journalists." Well, I don't either, I have a prejudice, but I told him Caputo's not a journalist. I found an old quarterly that no longer exists, I was going through it one night to see who was in there with me and what became of them, and there was Philip Caputo. He had some poems there, and the biographical thing said he was going off to Spain to write a book of poems and stories called *A Rumor of War.* My hunch is he made the right move in making it autobiographical. I like very much his second two novels. I am also a fan of Joseph

Wambaugh. A lot of people raise their eyebrows at that, but I think he's the only man who can tell us what it is really like to be a policeman in a large city, and in his first novel—he has the Watts riot from the point of view of the police, and it is wonderful. He does contrive, he is clumsy, but too many novels I read contrive and I think it is one of the built-in flaws of the novel. But he is honest and good. R. G. Vliet, a book called *Solitudes,* is one of the best American novels I have ever read. Nobody knows anything about it. Matter of fact, nobody knows anything about Paula Fox or Gina Berriault either.

TEK: Are you a voracious reader?

AD: I guess. I don't read as much as I want. I find that during the baseball season I tend to either watch or listen to the Red Sox. That's 162 games. I don't think I miss more than ten a year. I also find that sometimes when I am writing intensely, I don't have the kind of energy it takes to do good reading at night, and I will then turn to detective fiction which I do not think is a minor form. It just takes less *literary* intensity to read.

TEK: Which of your own fictions do you feel most satisfied with? Do you regret any?

AD: I guess I'm most satisfied with "Adultery." I don't know if it's the best, but it took four hundred typed pages, seven drafts, seventeen months of work spread over maybe two or three years. And I tried to put into there everything I knew about God, death, and women, and marriage. You ought to by now open a beer and say, "So why didn't you use the cover of a matchbook, asshole? Postage stamp?" But I am most satisfied with it, I guess, because it threw me off the saddle so many times and hurt me, and I kept giving up.

"Going Under" did the same thing to me. I kept quitting it. I feel very good about "The Pretty Girl" which wasn't even as hard to write, but it was very draining. I feel good about a story called "Waiting," which came from a hundred-page novella which was no good, and the total time on that seven-page story was fourteen months. And I feel a certain satisfaction for a story called "Delivering" because on a Sunday afternoon, I was taking my daughter Nicole to her riding lessons, and I decided to do something I rarely do and that is make up a story. And I decided to write about a little boy and no more sensitive little boys like my

116

autobiographical things, but a tough little boy—decided on the situation and the story was done, the first draft was done in five days, and it was just about complete.

Since *Voices from the Moon* is fairly recent, I feel good about that, but I even feel maybe better about something I was working on last January [1985] in Montpelier, a short novella of fifty-three pages called "Rose," which I think took more chances than a lot of other things I've done. I do not think I regret any of them. Some of them I don't like anymore, but that's because I was younger when I wrote them and could have done them better, so I don't put them in collections. I don't even regret *The Lieutenant* having been published. If I wrote that now, it would be a *good* hundred-page novella, but as it is, it is a weak two-hundred page novel, but there are real people in it so I don't regret it. If I regret, I don't send it off. By the time I send it off, I know I have taken it as far as I can, and there is really nothing more I can do with it. My only regret would be if I had been lazy or copped out.

TEK: What is your opinion of the so-called new fiction, metafiction, superfiction, surfiction, bossa nova, etc., by which I think of the work of writers like Barth, Barthelme, Coover, Gass, et al.?

AD: Well, these are writers I can't read. I have tried them all. I did like Coover's baseball book. It did not make me want to read any more Coover. I read two or three of Barthelme's books, and I gave up. Read some of Gass, gave up. I read *The End of the Road* by Barth, loved it, and then taught it and got angry. Seemed to me that in the abortion scene when she drowns in her own vomit, that we should have been weeping, and I don't like the comic distance, so I've never read a word of his since. But I can't call these people assholes because they write something that they feel, but I don't feel, something they like, but I don't like. I don't like their work, but I certainly respect their *doing* it. There is no way to criticize these people. I can't think they're phonies. I don't think they're dishonest. I think they are real artists. They work hard, and they are just doing something that doesn't interest me.

TEK: You give the rapist in "In My Life" the same surname as the antisexual priest in "If They Knew Yvonne." Is this just

117

coincidence? Do you choose your characters' names with significance and premeditation (e.g., as Barth's creative narrator in *The
Floating Opera* suggests that he is named Todd after the German
word for death) or do you let your unconscious select the names?

AD: That naming of the priest—Broussard—was just coincidence. There are so many Broussards in Louisiana, and I do tend
to forget my characters' names after I have named them. I have
a poor system for choosing names. Hardly any system at all. To
me, it is just a bother and something I got to get done to get the
story written.

TEK: You seem unconcerned about point-of-view shift in fiction. In "Separate Flights," you shift briefly from Beth to Peggy.
In "The Pretty Girl," you shift from a first-person Ray to a third-
person Polly back to a first-person Ray and end with a first-person
Alex.

AD: When I was in Iowa, I said to Dick Yates something about,
you can't split the point of view, and he said, "Why?" I didn't
have an answer. I was about twenty-eight then. He splits up point
of view a lot in his stories. I do it if another character suddenly
grabs me by the sleeve and says, I want to talk.

TEK: How often do you write? And how much do you get
done on a good day?

AD: I write seven days a week when I am writing something.
Not always. Things happen. Flu, colds. But that's my intention.
Sometimes I intentionally take time off. Right now I'm working
on a novella that I haven't worked on in over a week because I
went to the University of Arkansas, but I was going to take a
break from it anyway because I was starting to hate it, and the
vacation has done me good. I'm ready to get back to it. A good
day to me doesn't depend on the number of words, but on how
well they got written. Many days if I get a hundred words I'll
say that's fine. Other days I suddenly get 2,000. I probably average
three to five hundred.

Each morning I start by reading the last page I've written which
has been interrupted in half sentence, half scene, and I look at
the words in the margin. They tell me where the scene is going,
at least where it was going the day before; then I read from the
beginning making small changes, but mostly I read from the

beginning to get into the story. It is damn near impossible for me to just pick up where I left off because so much has happened from the time that I left off until the time that I have picked up again: dealing with the builder, the house, the phone, the child, hunting, having fun, drinking, who knows? When I write a novella, I only read the secton that I am working on or else it would take two hours to finally get back to work. Then, when I finish that first draft in long hand, I tape it, and I listen back, and I think the taping is very valuable because as you can see, by then I have read much of the story or novella, some passages, hundreds of times. Reading them aloud makes me concentrate more, and then listening back points out very quickly to me repetitions, lines of dialogue that I don't need, rhythms that I should work on, and then with luck, I type the final draft.

TEK: You have said that publishing in the *New Yorker* is like publishing in the Soviet Union.

AD: I think the *New Yorker* is, even more than college literature teachers, the worst influence there is on writers because of what I spoke about earlier—the reason that writers quit. One thing that will keep a writer going is to publish in a known magazine and be able to tell not only his mother, his father, his friends, people at a high school reunion, but at any bar in America, somebody says, "You write? Published anything?" "Yeah. *New Yorker*." "Oh! *New Yorker!*" It's our vanity, an understandable vanity and the *New Yorker* has that power. They also pay a lot, but as I say, how can you ever make enough money on a short story to sell a part of your soul? I know a story of a graduate student who sold his first story to the *New Yorker,* and they wanted him to rewrite it so that it was not in a southern voice, but in a neutral voice, and he did it, and I asked a friend why did he do it, and he said for thirty-five hundred. Well, I used to think that was the reason, but now I think he did it for the vanity (and again understandable vanity, but I use the word on purpose) so he would have evidence to show people that he is a writer. They are so dictatorial and use their power so much that I think they are capable of destroying a young writer's talent. I do not buy books of stories if the majority of them have been in the *New Yorker*. I buy Edna O'Brien's stories and some of them have been in there, but because she writes a lot about the flesh, generally the stories will be published in a slightly different form in the *New Yorker*. I think they are prissy, provincial, and totalitarian, and they can certainly destroy a writer. Who in the hell would want to sit around reading *New Yorker* stories for very long?

TEK: Have you experienced this from other periodicals as well? In general, has your published work been subjected to editorial suggestions or editing or nudgings?

AD: No, I haven't had any problems with publishing except one, and I do not consider the story published because of what happened. Philip [Philip G. Spitzer, Dubus's agent] sold "The Misogamist" to *Penthouse,* and when the story came out they had made eighty-five changes in fifteen pages. I wrote a very angry letter demanding a contract be signed that if they published "Killings," which had also been accepted, it be without change. So, of course, the editors sent "Killings" back, and that was the end of that. I will say this about the *New Yorker,* and I wrote this to the editor at *Penthouse*: they do have certain demands, I think totalitarian demands, but they are very gentlemanly about the way they go about them. I took back a story called "The Winter Father" [Interviewer's note: ultimately selected for publication in the annual volume of *Best American Short Stories*] because they called me and said that they wanted it and then sent a long letter asking for all these changes, and the letter literally gutted the story as well as removing the one use of the word "fuck" which I thought was a humorous use of it in the story. So I took the story back and *Sewanee Review* published it. Since I have only had seven, I think, out of forty-four stories in commercial magazines, I have had very small problems with that. I am generally in quarterlies. The thing about quarterlies is that usually either they like it or they don't, and if they do have suggestions, in my experience, they are either very wrong or very right. I think Hemingway said that about Ezra Pound.

TEK: What, if anything, other than the number of words, is the difference between a short story and a novella and a novelette and a novel? It seems to me that in your novellas (in which category I would also include "Separate Flights," although it is some thirty percent shorter than your other novellas), while the writing has that special tightness of a short fiction, you deal in greater breadth with your characters. For example, in "Separate

Flights," we see the sort of extended scenes with Beth that, e.g., we do not see of Miranda in "Miranda over the Valley." We live those months with Beth, while with Miranda, we live really only the period just after her abortion. Is this focus-span the essential difference between the forms? I mean, they are all short fiction anyway.

AD: In fact, I did an entire semester on the novella and short story and never did come up with a goddamn answer apart from your own—dealing in greater breadth with the characters. I'm glad you consider "Separate Flights" a novella. I always have, myself. I don't know the difference between a novelette and a novella. I know that the number of words is not the difference between a short story and a novel. In *The Lonely Voice,* Frank O'Connor says that some of Turgenev's novels are shorter than some of Chekhov's stories. I just threw that in to confuse the question. I don't believe in his theory concerning the passage of time. In my own experience, I write a novella when my characters demand more time on the page, more action, more exploration of their depth, more complexity. I would say that *Voices from the Moon* takes as long to read as *Play It as It Lays,* but the latter is a novel while the former is not. *Voices from the Moon* has the effect of a long short story. We see these people in a certain situation in a single day, but we don't quite know enough of their stories. I guess the novella becomes a novella when it wants to go more deeply into the characters and, very often, when it splits point of view.

TEK: I've heard various descriptions of the process of writing. Some say it is like feeling your way through a dark room, others like viewing a landscape in lightning. Hemingway, I believe, said that sometimes it is like drilling for oil, other times like mining coal. Strunk and White say it is "a question of learning to make occasional wing shots, bringing down the bird of thought as it flashes by." What is it for you? Meditation, inspiration, mining, drilling, trial and error?

AD: First, I would like to add a quote by Updike that I like very much. He said it was like driving at night. You can only see as far as your headlights are showing you, but if you keep driving you'll get there. For me, it is less inspiration or meditation than trying to see what you are trying to write, working very hard, trying to find the words and the rhythm to go with it.

TEK: Would you care to say a few words on your aesthetic principles here?

AD: A few words on my aesthetic principles here. Oh, shit, I am not sure what that means. I will answer the question pretending that I know what it means. I believe in absolute honesty, an easy word to throw around, but for example: in Chekhov's story "Peasants," a story written by a man who knew from the age of twenty-eight on that he had T.B. and, therefore, would not live long, there is a passage about a man in the household who is dying slowly, and Chekhov says, there comes a time in every household where there is someone dying when everyone wishes he would hurry up and get it done with, everyone except the children, only the children hope he won't. And I thought what a courageous line that was for him to write because his pen must have been flowing with the story when that insight came, and I like to imagine him suddenly being afraid and not wanting to continue that discovery, but then saying, Here I go, and continuing anyway. That is what I mean about honesty, not to be afraid of what your characters might discover for you. I think my job in writing a story is to create a human being and see how that person reacts to the world. It seems to me that when you are writing and when you are reading somebody who is really superb, you become like God, with that kind of compassion and love. You can become the character you are reading about and understand why he or she does everything he does, love that person, and then you close the book and you can return to the world of judgments and many times that world of judgments is a good place to return to. Even people who see movies come out with the complexity of this. In *Day of the Jackal*, for example, why was I all the time on the side of the assassin? You don't want de Gaulle shot, and you know he is not going to get shot, but you end up having complete empathy with the assassin. I think that is the magic. The writer takes two dimensions, paper and ink, and makes the reader, as Conrad said in that marvelous Preface to *The Nigger of the Narcissus*, "see." See, hell! Smell, taste, touch, hear! Brings the reader through his senses into the story so that he can *become* the character for a while and feel like that character. That is the magic.

TEK: That is the magic. What is the objective of fiction? What is fiction's highest aim and greatest accomplishment?

AD: I think the first objective of fiction is to give pleasure. That can be the kind of pleasure that makes the reader continue to turn the page, to want to find out what is going to happen. There are other forms of pleasure. There is the pleasure of insight, there is the pleasure of good company. I think that is the first objective. And without achieving that you can't get the rest. I think the next objective is through the pleasure to draw the reader out of himself or herself and take that reader into a search where both of you go in without knowing the answer. Look for some questions, watch some people dramatize the questions, live with those people and see if you and the reader can come up with an insight into the truth. That insight might be that there is no answer [chuckles], that insight might be terrible. So it is pleasurable, musical, enjoyable on a high level, and also sometimes on a level more prone to titillation, and in the process of this dance, we confront the difficulties of life and we try to understand, we confront mortality, we try to live other lives, to leap into the heart of another and understand.

An Interview with
Andre Dubus [1986]
*Patrick Samway**

Patrick Samway: What authors or works of literature have influenced you?

Andre Dubus: Chekhov the most. I cut my teeth on Hemingway, not stylistically or thematically, but because I did a research paper on him as an undergraduate. I learned a lot about the craft, not so much from reading his work, but about his approaches to writing. He gave me advice: Do physical exercise after writing and forget what you have written; don't think about it; let your subconscious think about it; always stop when you're doing well; save the rest for the next day and stop in midsentence (I still do that). I've violated that rule twice in my career; I went ahead and got too excited and I finished the scene of a story. And you know, you live another twelve lives before you get back to your desk the next day—with interruptions by your family, your friends, your enemies, and your bills. By the time I get back to my desk the next day, I don't even remember the story. Those two mornings after I violated that rule, I just walked up and down in the den all morning trying to remember what was supposed to happen next and attempting to get it in the story. It's wonderful advice. So I learned about writing from Hemingway.

Chekhov is the one that taught me to look more deeply, with more compassion and compression. Marvelous writer. I was writing my second novel when I read his story "Peasants." I was writing a novel that wasn't any good—just a bunch of scenes that anybody can put together. Something like some bad O'Hara. I read "Peasants" one afternoon after writing and I thought that was strange; Chekhov said he couldn't write a novel because he couldn't write narrative, but in this story he's covered in thirty pages an entire year and dealt with both one family and one

* This interview originally appeared in *America,* 15 November 1987. Reprinted with permission of America Press, Inc., 106 West 56th Street, New York, NY 10019. © 1986 All rights reserved.

peasant village—a microcosm of most of Russian society after the freedom of the serfs. Now how did he do that? Then I reread it and it's all scenes, almost. And I saw how he wrote them in scenes and compressed them into thirty pages and dealt with peasants, religion, booze, the innocence of children and their future as peasants. I threw away those two or three chapters and said, "It's time to learn how to write!" I began trying to learn how to write. That was in 1968 and I have been trying that ever since. And every time I read something great by Chekhov, I think, "Well, I've got a long way to go," which is the reason I keep doing it, I guess.

PS: What about some of the Southern authors?

AD: Faulkner—big influence. When I was younger, my inner thoughts were in Faulknerian rhythms. I never read Faulkner while I wrote. I still don't read his works while I'm writing. Only a couple of people I know have noticed some Faulknerian rhythms in my fiction. Richard Yates is one of them. Faulkner wrote action so well. He could create movement that is also suspended at the same time—and it's not slow motion. It's as though you can see each moment of the motion, but the motion is still moving, as in "Barn Burning" when Ab Snopes throws the rug on Major de Spain's porch, and Sarty Snopes is on the mule, kicking the mule, and Ab reaches out and pulls his hand back. Faulkner's rhythms show all the speed of throwing the rug and the rug thumping and the lights going on in the house and people coming down and the boy's fearful heart and the mule starting to move out. Faulkner has not really stopped the action because there is still motion going on. Perhaps the best example is in "Pantaloon in Black" when Rider kills the cheating Birdsong, who goes for his revolver as Rider takes out the razor to kill him; you get each detail of the movement—the razor blade in his fist and then its unfolding as it slashes Birdsong's throat before the blood even spurts. I know that's where my long sentences come from and the focus on detail when I'm writing some action. I have also been influenced by Gina Berriault and Nadine Gordimer.

PS: What about Flannery O'Connor?

AD: No, she frightens me. I don't read her much. I wish I had never read that quote of hers where she said that she writes about sacraments that nobody believes in. Every time I read her stories

I look for the sacraments and get lost in the story. A friend of mine gave me good advice, but I can't take it; he said, "Forget what Flannery O'Connor said, just read her stories." But I can't. I'm always looking around for baptisms and Communions. I wish she had never said what she said. I don't know. I have a story, "Miranda over the Valley," which is full of Catholic symbols and allusions, and yet few have mentioned them in critiques of this story. On the other hand, I hoped nobody would because they were for me.

PS: What about your own Catholicism? How important is that to you?

AD: I think it pervades my writing, because for a long time I wrote about people who had no relationship with the deity since I was curious about living like that. But I have always been a Catholic. I think my Catholicism has increased my sense of fascination and my compassion. When I write about Catholics, I get very excited because there are a lot of ethical problems Catholics can get into.

PS: For example?

AD: Well, if a person is a real Catholic, almost anything is an ethical problem, and that person can either resort to the rules the person has been taught, such as the Ten Commandments, the Six Commandments of the Church, or the person can move on to the New Testament and think about the ass being in the ditch. A Jesuit once said to me in high school: "You will never meet anybody who has committed a mortal sin. You have as much chance of doing that as you have of meeting someone who has committed a capital crime, because it is almost impossible to commit a mortal sin." Right? There has to be so much premeditation; you have to be as cold about it as a businessman or a hit man, and most people don't do that. That's why I think seven years is not a bad sentence for most murderers who kill a friend or someone in the family and would never do it again. I think most of them say, "Oh, my God," when they realize what they have done. Aren't ninety percent of our murders committed among family and friends?

PS: Would you identify yourself as a Catholic writer?

AD: Yes, always have.

PS: What does that mean in terms of your writing?

AD: Well, I see the whole world as a Catholic, so I can't help but see my characters through the eyes of a Catholic. The story I just finished, "Blessings," has, I think, a lot of religion in it, including secular sacraments. But, like many American families, these characters are not churchgoing people. The family in "Blessings" went through a good deal; there are a lot of blessings in the story.

PS: Updike said [in his review of] . . . *Voices from the Moon* that the Church still functions as a standard of measure. Do you agree with Updike's assessment?

AD: Yes, I do. I still think the main problem with the United States is that we lost God and we lost religion and we didn't replace God or religion with anything of value. It doesn't bother me if people (including my own children) don't have religion, as long as they replace it with a philosophy. We are raising my daughter Cadence as a Catholic. I like very much what the young priest said when he had all the parents of the children to be baptized over to the rectory the week before the baptism: "You are raising your child Catholic in the same way you are going to feed your children certain foods. It is good for the child, and at a certain age the child may say, 'I don't want this,' but you have to start it with a certain nutrition." Now if Cadence finds another philosophy later on, then I don't consider her religious training a failure. I don't consider her lost—a spiritual loss. This country hasn't found any philosophy except money—and selfishness. I find the United States a very nonspiritual country, and I think that is largely the problem. In fact, we might need an enforced agape for survival, and in this way maybe people will be good again. I've seen the whole of my fictive world through the eyes of someone who believes the main problem in the United States is that we have lost all spiritual values and not replaced them with anything that is comparable. We just pretend all this. We never have been a Christian country. As a matter of fact, there never has been a Christian country. Has there ever been a country that didn't kill its enemies, oppress the poor and bring the strong and rich to power? Well, it saddens me and angers me. Maybe that's why I'm fascinated by the mystics, those who transcend all that drowns me. The mystics remain in harmony with the earth and their fellow human beings and, yet, are above it all as they enjoy union with God. It's like an opera! It's beautiful!

Part 3

THE CRITICS

Introduction

Over the dozen years since Andre Dubus published his first collection of short fiction, critical attention has increased with the appearance of each new volume, both in quantity and in quality.

Surely, his books are and have always been reviewed, but in the course of the past few years, they have begun to attract analytical attention both volume for volume and for the body of his work as a whole. Thus, his work is brought not only to the attention of the general reading public, via the reviews appearing in daily newspapers and weekly book review sections, but also to the attention of an audience with a more systematic approach to literature, as well as to the creative community.

Joyce Carol Oates has more than once published reviews of Dubus collections whose quality of analysis gives a taste of a deeper critical perception than is generally found in the mass-market review. Likewise, in 1984, John Updike published a long essay-review of Dubus's *Voices from the Moon* which surveyed that very short novel's spiritual perimeters in a way that provides a valuable supplement for the casual reader of Dubus's fiction as well as for the more serious critic.

In 1987, *Delta,* the respected journal of American studies published at Université Paul Valéry in France, devoted an entire issue to a study of Dubus's work, departing from usual European critical behavior by including in the volume one of Dubus's short stories. With this publication, Dubus's fiction received its first systematic critical analysis: classical literary studies of several of his stories as well as an overview analysis of his themes, a lengthy interview, and an extensive bibliography. Following that, the weekly magazine *America* published an evaluation of his work at mid-career, and his most recent collection, *The Last Worthless Evening* (1986), attracted considerable attention among the nation's reviewers and critics. The esteem with which he is considered by his fellow writers of fiction was movingly demonstrated early in 1987 when a group of some of the nation's most prominent writers rallied on his behalf with a series of benefit readings and events to help defray the exorbitant medical expenses that had accrued when Dubus lost his leg coming to the aid of an injured motorist on a highway in Massachusetts. Among those who participated in the benefit were Kurt Vonnegut, Jr., John Updike, E. L. Doctorow, John Irving, Jayne Anne Phillips, Stephen King, and other prominent American writers—some of whom have also written about Dubus's fiction.

From the evaluations and reviews that have appeared over the past dozen years, I have tried to select the most penetrating and thought-provoking critiques of each of his collections as well as of his very short novel, *Voices from the Moon*, which Dubus himself describes as more like a very long story than a novel. Thus, I have included excerpts from pieces on each of his books (not including his earlier novel, *The Lieutenant*—republished in 1987 by Green Street Press, Boston—which is beyond the scope of this study), rounded off by an overview article by Joseph J. Feeney.

In making my selection, I have also tried to reach for a balancing out of my own views and viewpoints as expressed in the long essay with which this book begins, as well as to take into account views expressed by Andre Dubus in the interview section. Thus, I thought that Edith Milton's incisive comments on *Adultery and Other Choices* and John Updike's essay on *Voices from the Moon* were well worth including not only because of their intrinsic merit but also because of the balance and completion they bring to the book as a whole. Similarly, Joyce Carol Oates's comments on "The Pretty Girl" *(The Times Are Never So Bad)* seem a useful balance to mine, as they take the opposite point of departure, focusing more on Ray's brutishness than on Polly's vacuity.

I do not agree with everything that is written about Dubus's fiction in the excerpts that follow, but have included some simply *because* they express opinions I do not hold. Thus, I have included a longish excerpt from Julian Moynahan's largely unfavorable review of *Finding a Girl in America*. I have also tried to include a sense of the varied texture of thought and reaction that reviewers bring to their profession and to offer a contrast between the reviewer's and the critic's tasks and products: the best of the former are indistinguishable from the latter.

Introduction

It is hoped that these critical glimpses of Dubus's work will contribute to a more complete and objective critical survey of the short fiction of this contemporary American master of the genre.

[On *Separate Flights*]
*Joyce Carol Oates**

[Separate Flights] consists of a novella and seven short stories, each of which is a considerable achievement. Dubus's attentiveness of his craft and his deep commitment to his characters make the experience of reading these tales—which are almost without exception about lonely, pitiful people—a highly rewarding pleasure.

The author of a novel, *The Lieutenant,* published in 1967, Dubus writes in a vein that might be considered naturalistic, since he relies to a great extent upon charting his characters' experiences in a highly recognizable world, following them closely from one hour to the next, from one drink to the next, recording their unexceptional dialogues with one another, with great subtlety and tact pinpointing their rare moments of insight. All of his people are ordinary, though some have pretensions to being intellectual; many are trapped in stultifying marriages, though Dubus never suggests that they might have been capable of arranging other fates. Their arguments are familiar, even banal. Their defenses against the panic of dissolution are commonplace: drinking and adultery. But though Dubus's materials are naturalistic, and his style is never self-consciously lyric or poetic, one sees in the craftsmanship of the tales a rigorous paring-back, a concern for what is implied rather than stated, so that the stories as a whole— the eight "separate flights" of the collection—come to operate symbolically, to mean much more than they record. . . .

[On *Adultery and Other Choices*]
*Edith Milton**

[In *Adultery and Other Choices,* Dubus] examines a variety of relationships: family relationships, friendships between women,

---

* From a review that appeared in the *Ontario Review,* Fall–Winter 1976–77. Reprinted by permission.

* From a review that appeared in the *New Republic* 178, no. 5 (4 February 1978):33–35. Reprinted by permission of the *New Republic,* © 1978, the New Republic, Inc.

camaraderie between men, marriage, adultery. He writes of men and women in isolation from each other, and of men and women together. But, most particularly, he focuses on that monstrous division between the two, possibly conceived in nature, probably exaggerated by our culture and our values and described by Dubus in poignant detail as an integral part of his characters' daily lives. I can think of no-one who has drawn a more precise map of that no-man's land between the sexes than he has in his collection and in his earlier *Separate Flights*. And even in fiction written by women or journalistic accounts of how women live, it would be difficult to find as painful or as accurate a description of the futilities of keeping house as there is here in "Andromache" or in his earlier "We Don't Live Here Anymore."

The force of women absent is as palpable as their presence is. And the influences of marriage and passion are far less powerful in these stories than a more negative pressure, a vacuum in communication which begins as silence between husband and wife, and ends by inhaling husband, wife, children and society into a conspiracy of isolation. Where love, or even the desire for love, exists, life is sane; in "Graduation," for instance, where a much-used girl decides to become a virgin girl. Or in "Cadence," in which a young officer candidate for the Marine Corps counsels his friend, Paul, " 'to get a girl again. There's nothing like it . . . *Nothing*. It's another world, man' " Secure in his affections, he can afford to weigh his needs against the dehumanizing demands of the Corps, and leave. But Paul has long since been sucked into the void which existed between his parents. He has signed the Marine contract because he thinks it will please his father, and because the recruiting captain had appeared "like salvation . . . wearing the blue uniform and manly beauty that would fulfill Paul's dreams." In the confusion in which he lives, he needs the clear certainty of masculine order and approval, and the story ends as, his friend gone, he dissolves "into unity with the rest of the platoon."

Dubus himself spent five years in the Marine Corps, which exists in several of these stories as the antithesis of all things instinctual, sexual, and growing. It is not, in itself, really evil, or even inhuman. But its humanity springs from the need for silence, for peace from women and from life, and for the certain ritual which will replace the uncertainty of understanding. . . .

The best of the stories about Marine Corps life, and perhaps the best story in the collection is "Andromache," which makes explicit the conflict between the male compulsion for protocol, bravado and death, and the paradoxical female need to nurture and sustain, moreover, without disturbing the great male rituals. The story, which is written from the point of view of Ellen, a Marine Officer's wife, widowed by his latest quest for adventure, recalls their last Christmas together and her attempt to give a Christmas party for her husband's men. The party is a failure: the complex arrangement of Marine manners keeps the enlisted men from showing up. Ellen is hurt, but represses her anger at the waste of her food, her effort, in the all-encompassing need to be a good sport, to pull in her stomach, to mourn, finally, in silence. "Be a strong Marine," she says to her small son as he starts to cry at his father's funeral. While her daughter has already learned the lesson of self-repression, and, at the age of nine, knows as much as her mother does about control and selflessness in the face of the male needs and abandonments which have been the lot of military wives since Andromache.

But by extension, all wives are military wives, and the Marines only the most potent of those institutions in which a man can feel his manhood safe from interruption. There is some security even in the lesser sports. In poker, for instance, and in golf. Men jog together to express their friendship and to get away from their wives, and though families speak often to each other with affection, they speak around secrets and gaps of the unspeakable. . . .

Ambivalence is the pivot of Dubus's world, which is a world in splinters, where men and women face in opposite directions, and Catholic mother and Protestant father do not meet sufficiently even to disagree. A man, to feel himself a man, must sacrifice himself on the altar of masculine ritual, and even adultery stems from routine and a sense of what one owes oneself more than it does from real feeling.

It is impossible to escape the suspicion that most of these stories have an autobiographical source, especially those in which Dubus patently disparages the masculine ideals of the protagonist. Most of the women emerge triumphantly human: Ellen of "Andromache," Bobbie, the restored virgin of "Graduation," and Louise,

"The Fat Girl," who goes on a diet just long enough to discover that fat is what she is, and that any love worth the name can find her under the blubber. These women, and Paul's unposturing, gently failing friends, are the valiant of the earth: the others are oppressed by their maleness as by a burden. It is his ability at once to understand the strong and to exonerate the silly which makes Dubus's writing enormously engaging.

The title story, "Adultery," is the last and longest of the book, and in it Dubus tries to arrive at some sort of accommodation for all the fragments of his universe. The accommodation is uncomfortable and difficult, for the reader, I think, as well as for the characters, since it invokes a sexual answer for a spiritual need, and a spiritual answer for a sexual one; a combination which presents notable problems of perspective also in D. H. Lawrence, of whom Dubus often reminds one. . . .

There is no question that Dubus is at his best when he examines the shards of his particular universe, when he charts the islands of domestic and military routine which define the seas of incomprehension on which his characters live. Putting the pieces together, he is less convincing; one feels the scale of Eternity jarring against the smallness of his people.

But Dubus is an exact and a compelling writer. The power of all these stories is very great, and the direction of the last is interesting. One wonders of what Dubus may be capable when he knows the path better, when he can describe the way to salvation with the same easy authority with which he describes the mined waste-land which stretches between lives.

[On *Adultery and Other Choices*]
*Frances Taliaferro**

Andre Dubus is a skillful and temperate writer. *[Adultery and Other Choices]* takes some getting used to. As when a harpsi-

* From a review included in "Books in Brief," *Harper's Magazine.* Copyright © 1978 by *Harper's Magazine.* All rights reserved. Reprinted from the January issue by special permission.

chordist opens his recital with sounds that seem unbearably faint
after the noise outside, Dubus invites us into a world of quiet
melodies. Gradually, the ear learns to hear them. When Dubus
writes about growing up in Louisiana, he finds nothing of the
Southern Gothic. These fine stories are the equivalent of Hopper
landscapes, anywhere in small-town America. . . . People play
golf, go to barbecues, have fights around the Coke machine at
school. The mystery is out of all proportion to the events. "Contrition," the best story, is ostensibly about ten-year-old Paul and
his brief involvement with the French horn. In fact it says all
that ever need be said about the pain of family love. The title
story, "Adultery," takes as its epigraph a quotation from Simone
Weil: "Love is a direction and not a state of the soul." Dubus
constructs a disturbing spiritual framework that mocks the ac-
customed tackiness of the subject. Less good are several rather
trite stories set in the U.S. Marine community. This collection is
uneven, but Dubus at his best can evoke thoughts that lie too
deep for tears.

[On *Finding a Girl in America*]
*Julian Moynahan**

[In *Finding a Girl in America*] Mr. Dubus's regional ambiance is
the northeast corner of Massachusetts, a district comprised by
Haverhill and Newburyport, Plum Island and Salisbury Beach,
and crossed by the Merrimack and Parker Rivers. It used to be
considered Marquand country. Mr. Dubus, however, is much more
focused on the life of the lower middle-class and blue-collar
families than the master of Wickford Point ever was. Updike
country lies immediately to the south. It turns out that Mr. Dubus's
stories are just as much into divorce and adultery and the sorrows
of children putting up with quarreling, betraying, separating parents
as Updike's stories of well-educated affluent Boston commuters
and professional people are.

* From "Hard Lives," the *New York Times Book Review,* 22 June 1980, 12.
Copyright © 1980 by the New York Times Co. Reprinted by permission.

Julian Moynahan

The typical Dubus male grows up in a decaying, contracting small industrial city like Haverhill, or a bypassed port such as Newburyport, has boyish adventures at the seaside and develops a lifelong passion for the Red Sox—those heartbreakers!—sees something of the world during a peacetime stint in the Marines during the mid-1950s, then settles back into the home region where he may develop problems with drink, job or with the drive for liberation and autonomy of his womenfolk. A variant of this type is the writer figure appearing in the title story, whose social origins are the same but who tries to live the freer life of the artist without betraying or denying his class and regional roots. Yet this longer narrative is a failure precisely because Mr. Dubus and his hero, Hank Allison, hold such a self-centered, self-indulgent view of the artist and his responsibilities.

The best stories are those in which there are no overt or concealed self-portraiture and artist-portraiture: for instance, "Waiting," a brief vignette of a cocktail bar waitress, widowed since the Korean War, who works near Camp Pendleton, California, and keeps faithful to her soldier husband's memory, even as she turns forty and must patch together a sex life out of occasional one-night stands with Marine non-coms.

Even better is "Delivering," about two brothers who wake up on the Sunday morning on which their mother left their father and them for good, after a night of parental fighting and drinking in the kitchen. They go out together to deliver their paper route, spend the rest of the morning at the beach, then return to the house to pick up the pieces of their own lives and their father's. The story is notable for its insight into what these decent boys, fifteen and twelve, really worry about, are angered by, and the remarkable amount of family trauma they can cope with. Without omitting any scabrous details—the kitchen at dawn full of empty liquor bottles, spoiled food and overflowing ashtrays, the father overheard slapping the mother and his loud weeping after she walks out to join her lover—"Delivering" somehow delivers an endorsement of the American family, from the standpoint of the children's need for it to survive, that is touching and oddly optimistic.

Two stories of violence, "Townies" and "Killings," work pretty well—though I wish Mr. Dubus's attitude toward the instance of

139

murderous vigilantism and blood feud in the latter came through more clearly. . . .

Mr. Dubus has mastered many of the tools and techniques of his craft, though he pointlessly splits infinitives, starts far too many nonsentences with "Which," and uses current cant words like "judgmental" and "vulnerable" without irony. But he really runs off the track with "Finding a Girl in America," an unmotivated, histrionic tale about an aging divorced writer and writing teacher at a small college for women.

Hank Allison writes, runs, drinks, reads, has a teen-age daughter and a teen-age mistress whom he has recruited, as he goes each year, from among his younger students. On this day he is told by his current mistress Lori how last year's mistress had become pregnant, probably with Hank's child, and got an abortion.

Over the next many hours Hank howls, blubbers, vomits, whines to his ex-wife, and generally chews the scenery because he really wanted that kid, see? *She* would have been a girl to replace the daughter now growing up and to go with Lori, whom he now plans to marry. And of course there is no need to be concerned about Monica's health and happiness, because she was always "angry" and "hysterical." At one point, when Hank lectures Lori about their relationship, he uses the pronoun "I" twenty-one times and "you" six times. If she had a decent regard for herself and her sex she'd tell him to get lost.

[On *We Don't Live Here Anymore: The Novellas of Andre Dubus*]
*Harriett Gilbert**

[Dubus writes about] relentless wars of attrition (usually between spouses) conducted with fists, with a gun, and with words, with whatever's lying around. *We Don't Live Here Anymore* is very much from the school that *Granta* christened Dirty Realism. Its

* From "States of Desire," *New Statesman* 108, no. 2799, 9 November 1984, 32. Reprinted by permission.

deft, economical, concentrated prose exposes an introverted USA of six-packs, all-day television, fishing-and-shooting trips for the men, bourbon numbness for the women. But it's also after something different. Almost alone among books by men, from *any* literary school, it's questioning what being "male" really means.

In the first story, "The Pretty Girl," there's an obvious distance between the author and the flailing, iron-pumping, wife-raping Ray, who can't understand why his pretty little Polly has left him and won't come back. In the three linked novellas that follow, however, the men's attempts to make some sense of manhood, marriage, parenthood, love, women's and their own sexuality, have the engrossing complexity of something very immediate. Structurally, there are long, looping flashbacks that dissipate the stories' momentum, while the final novella ties up its ends in a disappointingly cozy little bow. None of this should distract from the book's honest strengths.

[On *The Times Are Never So Bad*]
*Joyce Carol Oates**

Andre Dubus's fourth collection of short stories derives its title from a remark by St. Thomas More with which no one would wish to quarrel: "The times are never so bad but that a good man can live in them." Though Mr. Dubus's characters are not precisely "good"—most of them perform criminal actions of one kind or another—we are allowed to see how they define themselves as other than merely "bad" through the author's extraordinary sympathy with them; he has a gift for conveying, with a wonderful sort of clairvoyance, their interior voices. Indeed, the strongest pieces in the collection—the novella and the final story, "A Father's Story"—are really triumphs of voice, memorable for their resonance.

* From "People to Whom Things Happen," the *New York Times Book Review,* 26 June 1983. Copyright © 1983 by the New York Times Co. Reprinted by permission.

The Critics

The fifty-six-page novella, "The Pretty Girl," ranks with the strongest stories in Mr. Dubus's earlier collections. . . . It may be the most compelling and suspenseful work of fiction this author has written. The "pretty girl" of the title is a young woman named Polly, separated from her husband for reasons mysterious to him but quite clear to us and fated to be his killer. She is a near-alcoholic in her mid-twenties, said to be intelligent but in fact sleepwalking through life, oddly alone but rarely feeling herself lonely. Polly's very prettiness estranges her from women who might otherwise be friends. . . .

Vivid as Polly is in all her soiled innocence, her former husband Ray is even more forceful. He commits brutish actions—raping Polly at knife-point, badly injuring her lover, sprinkling gasoline around her house at night and lighting it—but he isn't wholly a brute. Mr. Dubus builds his portrait of Ray in a slow, detailed, fastidious way, allowing us to hear Ray's voice and to foresee his fate without quite passing judgment. Indeed, Mr. Dubus often seems to be arguing in these stories, judgment is beside the point: Things happen to people and are rarely willed by them. Polly's and Ray's voices contend in the novella, and though Polly triumphs—if her desperate act of murder can be so described— it is Ray whose voice stays with us, plodding, self-justifying, "logical." He drinks a great deal; he lifts weights compulsively; he would have been at peace with the world, except for his wife's sudden defection. . . . Ray dies not knowing why Polly has stopped loving him, when, after all, he is so convinced he loves her.

Set beside the unhurried precision of "The Pretty Girl," most of the other stories are somewhat under-developed, even sketchy. In "Bless Me, Father," a college-girl discovers that her father is committing adultery and shames him into giving up his mistress. In "Leslie in California," a young wife broods over the fact that her husband, whom she loves and depends upon, has blackened her eye in one of his drunken frenzies—and not for the first time. In the rather bleak and atonic "The New Boy," a teenager, whose father has left his family, drifts almost brainlessly into self-destructive acts of vandalism in the company of a psychotic youth. These are spare pieces of fiction, wilfully pruned, it seems, of the rich and idiosyncratic details that elsewhere make Mr. Dubus's writing so good; they read rather more like excerpts from longer works than stories complete in themselves.

Andre Dubus's fiction is perhaps an acquired taste, for his characters are resolutely ungiving and uncharming. Most of them drink beer in vast quantities and contend with periodic hangovers; all of them are addicted to one thing or another, which Mr. Dubus examines with an extraordinary sympathy—drinking, smoking, black coffee, Quaaludes. When their various addictions fail they tend to think, like Ray, "It's time to do some more terrorizing." In the main, however, their addictions comfort them and give them reasons to keep on living. Where another writer might dramatize his characters' plights in order to reveal and exorcise their strategies of delusion, Mr. Dubus has other intentions. Like the hard-drinking protagonist of "The Captain," who has survived an unspeakably grueling experience in the war, he has learned "of how often memory lies, and how often the lies are good ones."

[On *The Times Are Never So Bad*]
*Brian Stonehill**

Imagine you're a character in one of Andre Dubus's short stories— say, the adolescent Walter in "The New Boy." You're swimming in your wealthy Boston family's backyard pool, having invited the new boy in the neighborhood to come over. Suddenly he dives in on top of you, hooks his arm around your neck from behind, and starts to drag you under. You have to fight to get free, and in a few minutes you will show your displeasure by bloodying his nose. But then you will be friends.

That is how Dubus's stories affect the reader. Violence pounces upon us without warning, and drags us to where we think we cannot breathe. It's not "pleasant," not "amusing." But it turns out, with Dubus, that we *can* breathe in his distorted underwater world, and there is much to see.

Dubus's handsome fourth collection of fiction bears an epigraph about violence from Flannery O'Connor, and in fact Dubus resembles the great Southern Gothic writer in his power, his ability

* Copyright 1983 by Brian Stonehill. Reprinted by permission. This essay originally appeared in the *Los Angeles Times Book Review,* 14 August 1983.

to command our attention. Each story opens with a nearly irresistible hook. "I don't know how I feel till I hold that steel." The stories welcome you in, entice you skillfully.

Dubus resembles O'Connor, too, in his concern with matters spiritual. Even more explicitly than she, he focuses on the place of faith and grace in a Catholic heart. He hunts for purity's place in all of this, and is too clever and clear-sighted to settle for an easy answer.

Where he differs, though, is in his view of the sexes. O'Connor was a lumper; Dubus is a splitter. As if conditioned by life in a war zone, Dubus sees the sexes as *us* vs. *them*. We men understand each other. Women get a little weird. They'll kill you if they get the chance. In the world of *macho* letters, there's no better model of this skewed view than Ernest Hemingway, and sometimes Dubus sounds like an entry in a bad-Hemingway contest. . . .

Men in this world brawl among themselves, rape their wives, rescue their daughters; women cuddle and kill their men. What can a poor boy do? Young Walter strikes a blow for *macho* rule by disposing of his mother's and his two sisters' birth control devices. That's all he *can* do. His older counterparts will get themselves in trouble and even killed on account of women. . . .

The teller of "A Father's Story" mentions and then enacts "the necessity and wonder of ritual." For him it means talking to God, and imagining His response. Fiction—particularly short fiction, which suffers unjustly from publishers' neglect—offers itself as a similarly vital ritual. It talks to us and imagines our responses. Dubus at his best does this very well.

Memory is the lens that lets us look out of a single event across the whole of the life that led to it; language is the light that brings it to mind's eye. . . . These stories have a life of their own, even if that life is, I hope, grimmer than our own. The words get into our imagination and somehow spring to life there; then they tramp into the memory and so stay with us. . . .

For all our skepticism of language, stories such as these remain the wisest and most thorough way we have of absorbing distant life. The richer we are in rituals, the brighter the flow of that gemlike flame.

John Updike

[On *Voices from the Moon*]
*John Updike**

As a writer, Andre Dubus has come up the hard way, with a resolutely unflashy style and doggedly unglamorous, unironical characters. These characters have tended to live in the north of Boston's urbane suburbs, in the region of Massachusetts bordering southern New Hampshire, from Newburyport to Haverhill, the city where Mr. Dubus now resides. The Merrimack Valley was the New World's first real industrial belt, and has been economically disconsolate for decades; the textile mills moved south, and then foreign imports undermined the leather and shoe factories. But life goes on, and life's gallant, battered ongoingness with its complicated fuelling by sex, religion, and liquor, constitutes his sturdy central subject, which is rendered with a luminous delicacy and a certain attenuating virtuosity in his new, very short novel, *Voices from the Moon.* . . .

The title comes from a poem by Michael Van Walleghen, mentioning "the several voices / Which have called to you / Like voices from the moon." The voices, presumably, are the six characters whose points of view and interior monologues the reader shares in the course of nine chapters. The action takes place in one day, and its principal event is the announcement by Greg Stowe, the forty-seven-year-old owner of two ice-cream stores, that he intends to marry his twenty-five-year-old former daughter-in-law, Brenda. Along with Greg's and Brenda's, we get to eavesdrop on the thoughts and perceptions of Joan, Greg's first wife; Larry, Brenda's first husband and Greg's older son; Carol, Greg's twenty-six-year-old daughter, and Richie, his twelve-year-old son. The story, really, is Richie's; we begin and end in his mind, early in the morning and late at night, and two more chapters trace, as the day progresses, his inner turmoil over his confusing proposed change within his family. He has been living with his father, visiting his mother in the nearby town of Amesbury, and often seeing his brother, who will now, he fears, shun the new household.

* From "Ungreat Lives," the *New Yorker,* 4 February 1985, 94, 97–98. Reprinted by permission; © 1985 John Updike. Originally in the *New Yorker.*

Richie is a normal-appearing boy—"a lean suntanned boy . . . neither tall nor short"—with the heart of a saint. He likes horseback riding and softball and cross-country skiing well enough but the Catholic Church forms his deepest preoccupation and solace. He attends Mass, by himself, almost every morning, and hopes to become a priest.

> Now Father Oberti lifted the chalice and Richie imagined being inside of him, feeling what he felt as the wine he held became the Blood of Christ. My Lord and my God, Richie prayed, striking his breast, immersing himself in the longing he felt there in his heart: a longing to consume Christ, to be consumed through Him into the priesthood, to stand some morning purified and adoring in white vestments, and to watch his hands holding bread, then God.

On a different plane of attraction from Father Oberti stands Melissa Donnelly, who is three months older than Richie and, at barely thirteen, one of the youngest temptresses in fiction since Nabokov's Lolita. In the course of the never violent events of this summer day—a day, like most, of modest revelations and adjustments—we see Richie's priestly vocation just perceptibly erode. Though the novel bares a number of hearts, in a range of tough, detached, and even perverse adult attitudes, its supreme and presiding achievement is its convincing portrait of his benign male child, from whom the trauma of parental divorce and the instruction of the Church have elicited a premature manliness. When his father asks him his opinion on the coming marriage, Richie merely says, "I want you to be happy," and the gritty older man has the grace to flush and become momentarily speechless.

A dramatically versatile overview, as in *Voices from the Moon*, risks reminding us too much of the overviewer. Mr. Dubus has taken special care with his three women, and has much to tell us about female sexuality and, contrariwise, the female lust for solitude: Joan, having "outlived love," rejoices in her manless apartment and the comradely after-hours company of her fellow-waitresses. Carol and Brenda also live alone, but have not yet outlived love, and seem therefore a bit doomed; one of the novel's theological implications is that in seeking relief from solitude we sin, and fall inevitably into pain. Joan reflects that "Richie had always been solitary and at peace with it," so it is with a distinct sense of loss that the reader sees him, at the end, turn toward a human comforter. All three women, though assigned different attributes, are given neither much physical presence nor a palpable distinctness at the core; all three are too ready, perhaps, to train their thoughts upon the bumbling, rugged wonder of the masculine. Brenda fondly marvels at the way male friends never really talk about their lives, standing together at bars for hours, and how they fight "like two male dogs" and how "also like dogs they would not hurt each other." And Carol, looking at her own father, comfortably sees "in his lowered face, and his smile, that look men wore when they knew they were bad boys yet were loved by a woman anyway." For Dubus's men, as for Raymond Carver's not dissimilar quasi-blue-collar, six-pack-packing heroes, women tend to loom larger than life and to merge into one big, treacherous, irresistible lap. Carol, whose daughterliness cuts across the great sexual division, and Larry, who by a twist in his nature somewhat straddles it, are relatively cloudy stops in Mr. Dubus's tour of the Stowe family. Of his nine chapters, too many end with an embrace, with or without tears, and sometimes the language becomes overemotional: "And in the sound of his expelled breath Greg heard defeat and resignation, and they struck his heart a blow that nearly broke him, nearly forced him to lower his face into his hands and weep." The language can also wax portentous: "Because when you fought so much and so hard, against pain like this . . . so you could be free to lie in the shade of contentment and love, the great risk was that you would be left without joy or passion, and in the long evenings of respite and solitude would turn to the woman you loved with only the distracted touch, the distant murmurs of tired responsibility." At the opposite pole, the demythologizing simplicities of Hemingway intrude: "He crouched to lock the rear wheel and was very hungry and hoped his father was making pancakes." And there is an excess of procedural detail, relating not to catching fish in the Big Two-Hearted River but to food preparation along the Merrimack: pancakes and bacon, tequila, lunch for the diet-conscious, vodka with onions and pepper—we learn how to prepare and consume them all. These characters are well catered to.

Yet Mr. Dubus's willingness to brood so intently above his

disturbed, divorced, mostly lapsed Catholics lends his survey an aerial quality, an illusion of supernatural motion, that reminds us of what people used to read novels for. How rare it is, these days, to encounter characters with wills, with a sense of choice. Richie and his father both muster their inner strengths, make resolves, and grieve over their decisions. The most threatening opponents, Greg believes, are those without bodies: "Self-pity, surrender to whatever urged him to sloth or indifference or anomie or despair." In this book, the streams of consciousness are channeled by mental exertion; the mind is a garden where some thoughts and impulses can be weeded out and others encouraged. Purity beckons everyone to a clean place described by the epigraph: ". . . No, there is / Nothing left for you / But to stand here / Full of your own silence / Which is itself a whiteness / And all the light you need."

Greg daydreams of walking beside an unspoiled Amazon, "where each step was a new one, on new earth." Brenda renounces promiscuity, and Joan has walked away from motherhood, at enduring cost to herself; when the opportunity arises to "tell one of her children something she knew, and to help the child," she seizes it, spelling out for Larry, who feels humiliated by losing his ex-wife to his father, the way in which the wound will heal and life will go on. For Jack Kerouac, another Franco-American from the Merrimack Valley, Roman Catholicism had dwindled to a manic spark, a frenetic mission to find the sacred everywhere; for Mr. Dubus, amid the self-seeking tangle of secular America, the Church still functions as a standard of measure, a repository of mysteries that can give scale and structure to our social lives. The family and those intimate connections that make families are felt by this author as sharing the importance of our souls, and our homely, awkward movements of familial adjustment and forgiveness as being natural extensions of what Pascal called "the motions of Grace."

. . . This small novel . . . of slight movements within the heart yields morals that are modest, even bleak. . . . Joan tells Larry, "So when I'm alone at night—and I love it, Larry—I look out my window, and it comes to me: we don't have to live great lives, we just have to understand and survive the ones we've got." Relief from what Ibsen, in "The Wild Duck," called "the claim of the ideal" is being prescribed. "Oh, life would be quite tolerable, after all," Ibsen's Dr. Relling concludes, "if only we could be rid of the confounded duns that keep on pestering us, in our poverty, with the claim of the ideal." . . . But have the people of *Voices from the Moon* been trying, except for Richie, to lead "great lives"? Joan's statement has this context: Larry is a dancer, and his mother has just asked him why he doesn't leave the Merrimack Valley and throw himself at New York. He won't, she knows. So, since more people, through humility or inability, must live in the Merrimack Valleys of the world than on the heights, she says what she can, which isn't much—for what does it mean, really, to "understand" and "survive" your own life? Religious resignation without religion is cold comfort. Traditional preachments promised a better life, an afterlife or a Messiah-led revolution. Joan promises nothing, and Mr. Dubus promises little more, though he does imagine Richie lying on his back on "the soft summer earth" and feeling himself sink down into a normal human life, still "talking to the stars."

But then Richie is only twelve, years short of such concrete realizations as "Everyone wants to be alive, nobody wants to be dead. Everything else is a lie."

[On *The Last Worthless Evening*]
*James Yaffe**

Andre Dubus writes novellas—long stories that run about a fifth to a third the length of ordinary novels—and this probably accounts for the fact that, after seven distinguished books, he hasn't yet achieved a large readership or widespread critical recognition. This is a pity, because on the strength of his eighth book, *The Last Worthless Evening,* I have no hesitation in calling him one of the best writers of fiction in America today.

The Last Worthless Evening contains four novellas and two short stories. . . . [about] . . . Catholics, struggling to reconcile the remnants of religious training and belief with their sexual

* From the *Denver Post,* 7 December 1986. Reprinted by permission.

desires, their need for money, their yearning to find some kind of happiness and purpose in a bewildering and hostile world.

This struggle is at the center of every one of the stories in this collection, but oddly enough it doesn't make them depressing. Dubus is a rarity among contemporary writers: He is tough and realistic, he sees everything that is alienating and dehumanizing in the modern world, but somehow he also manages to be an optimist. Not about what's likely to happen to individual human beings—many of his characters suffer terrible fates—but about the ability of the human spirit to show courage and grace in the most unpromising circumstances.

"Deaths at Sea" shows a couple of young Navy officers, white and black, forging some kind of genuine love and understanding in an atmosphere of race prejudice; "Molly" opens up the posibility for motherhood and family happiness in a young girl whose sexual development has been forced and distorted by a world and a mother laboring under the burdens of the new sexual freedom.

It is Dubus's special triumph that he never sentimentalizes these optimistic insights. His characters never achieve transcendence easily or cheaply; in fact, there is always some ambiguity about whether they have achieved it at all, or whether any individual victory can be generalized to apply to other human beings. We can't be entirely sure what the girl in "Molly" will do with her life after the story ends, or how long the friendship between the white Navy officer and the black Navy officer will last.

Dubus's artistic method—the fact that he writes novellas rather than short stories—seems designed to reinforce this ambiguity. He starts off with ideas that most writers might develop in terms of one simple vivid scene or incident. Without ever betraying the vividness of that incident—and Dubus is brilliant at recreating action, making us see and hear what's happening—he introduces into each of his novellas a number of apparently irrelevant events, anecdotes that the narrator remembers and tells us about through long digressions from the central action.

In "Rose," for example, the story of the woman with the child-beating husband is prefaced by the narrator's memory of a pathetic recruit who flunked out of Marine officer's training. It is only at the very end of the novella that we see the point of this digression, the way in which it complicates our feelings about the central incident. And the moment when we see this connection is supremely moving and aesthetically satisfying. Through this method, Dubus has made the idea yield a significance and dramatic power that most writers never would have found in it.

[Andre Dubus at Fifty]
*Joseph J. Feeney**

Blurbs and pictures on the dustjackets of his books seem to tell it all. He looks like a teamster or a bear-hunter: solid build, bushy beard, blue cap marked "Captain," jeans with a wide leather belt. He is a baseball addict, was a Marine for over five years, carries an axehandle in his car trunk and has a strong social conscience. He calls himself a "cradle-Catholic," often attends daily Mass, has been married three times and likes vodka with pepper grains. He gives salty interviews, writes careful prose, creates superb stories and shows unusual insight into women and boys in his fiction. He has been awarded Guggenheim and National Endowment for the Arts fellowships, dislikes James Joyce and has published stories in such places as the *New Yorker,* the *Paris Review, Harper's* and the *Sewanee Review.* His work is admired by Joyce Carol Oates and John Updike, has almost a cult following and yet is not well known.

Yet a biographical sketch of Andre Dubus would not be complete without one more detail. On July 23, 1986, while being a Good Samaritan to a man and a woman who had been involved in an accident on Route 53 north of Boston, Mr. Dubus was himself seriously injured and spent his fiftieth birthday in Massachusetts General Hospital comforted by his wife Peggy and their daughter Cadence. Supported by his family, his friends and his faith, he is determined to continue his creative writing and not allow himself to be daunted by any physical disability.

Born in Louisiana on Aug. 11, 1936, and living now in blue-collar Haverhill, Mass., Andre Dubus (pronounced Duh-*beusse*)

* From "Poised for Fame: Andre Dubus at Fifty," by Joseph J. Feeney, S. J., professor of English at Saint Joseph's University, Philadelphia. This essay originally appeared in *America,* 15 November 1987.

The Critics

has sprinkled bits of his past in his novels, short stories and
novellas. He writes about boyhood in small Louisiana cities, life
in the Marine Corps (on an aircraft carrier, a Pacific island and
West Coast bases), graduate school in Iowa, and college teaching,
marriage, children and "Ronnie D's" bar in the Merrimack Valley
near Haverhill. Out of this material he has already gotten nine
books: first a novel, *The Lieutenant* (1967), then four books of
stories, *Separate Flights* (1975), *Adultery & Other Choices* (1977),
Finding a Girl in America (1980), and *The Times Are Never So
Bad* (1983). Each of these collections included a novella—his best
form. And these four novellas, interrelated by recurring characters,
were published together in his sixth book, *We Don't Live Here
Anymore* (1984). The same year brought Dubus's superb *Voices
from the Moon,* a well-reviewed novel that views the same events
from six different perspectives. In 1984, he also published, in
limited edition, *Land Where My Fathers Died,* a thirty-seven-page
detective story of multiple perspective that also appeared in the
magazine *Antaeus.* Dubus's ninth book, *The Last Worthless Evening* (1986), is a collection of six short stories and novellas.

What does he write about? The best answer, I suppose, is marriages—their relationships, tensions and adulteries—and families,
especially the children. Dubus is a careful observer, and his perceptions of human feelings, attitudes and reactions are unusually
acute. Furthermore, as an artist, he can communicate these perceptions through carefully invented characters, situations, events,
dialogues and phrases. Take as an example this description of a
thirty-six-year-old man visiting his young lover in "Going Under":
"In her purple sweater and pants she is lovely, and he presses
his face into her shoulder, her hair, he is squeezing her and her
heels lift from the floor, then he kisses her and breathes from
deep in her throat the scorched smell of dope. He looks at her
green eyes: they are glazed and she is smiling, but it is a smile
someone hung there: Miranda is someplace else."
    Dubus's fiction tells about the hope of love and the lack of
love and the death of love. His characters wish terribly for lifelong
love but, to their sadness, rarely find it; rather, in Dubus's fiction
as in American society, all too many marriages and families fail.
"All adultery is a symptom," he writes, and in his best work he
examines the illnesses of American marriages and families and

Joseph J. Feeney

the underlying "failures of the human heart." In *Voices from the Moon,* he even describes a shattered family trying to formulate their own stumbling explanations for their pains and loss: "The trouble was love," or "It's divorce that did it," or "She had outlived love." In other stories and novellas certain characters are even able to foresee the collapse of love. In "Separate Flights," Beth Harrison, who has long stopped loving her insurance-man husband, muses about her young daughter: "Now her seventeen-year-old, Peggy, was in love and she liked to talk about her plans, with this grown-up tone in her voice, and there was nothing to do but listen to her, not as you listen to a child who wants to be a movie star, but to a child whose hope for friends or happiness is so strong yet futile that you know it will break her heart."

The divorced fathers, too, grieve for their lost marriages and wounded children. In "The Winter Father," Peter Jackman remembers: "He and Norma had hurt each other deeply, and their bodies had absorbed the pain. . . . Now fleshless they could talk by phone, even with warmth, perhaps alive from the time when their bodies were at ease together. He thought of having a huge house where he could live with his family, seeing Norma only at meals, shared for the children, he and Norma talking to David and Kathi; their own talk would be on extension phones in their separate wings; they would discuss the children, and details of running the house. This was of course the way they had finally lived, without the separate wings, the phones. And one of their justifications as they talked of divorce was that the children would be harmed, growing up in a house with parents who did not love each other, who rarely touched and then by accident. There had been moments near the end when, brushing against each other in the kitchen, one of them would say: "Sorry." And in a passage I find hard to forget, the same Peter Jackman, with rueful humor, epitomizes the awkwardness of the divorced father who has visitation-rights every Saturday: "He thought of owning a huge building to save divorced fathers. Free admission. A place of swimming pool, badminton and tennis courts, movie theaters, restaurants, soda fountains, batting cages, a zoo, an art gallery, a circus, aquarium, science museum, hundreds of restrooms, two always in sight, everything in the tender charge of women trained in first aid and Montessori, no uniforms, their only style warmth and cheer."

Dubus can also be harsh in his honesty. In the novella "We Don't Live Here Anymore," the narrator, Jack Linhart, is having an affair with his best friend's wife, Edith Allison. As they are lying together, Jack recalls an evening when he and his wife Terry were with the Allisons and two other couples: "Once at a party Terry was in the kitchen with Edith and two other wives. They came out grinning at the husbands: their own, the others. They had all admitted to shotgun weddings. That was four years ago and now one couple is divorced, another has made a separate peace, fishing and hunting for him and pottery and college for her; and there are the Allisons and the Linharts. A deck-stacking example, but the only one I know." Then Edith tells him a truth about her husband, her daughter, and herself:

> "He needs us, Sharon and me, but he can't really love anyone, only his work, and the rest is surface."
> "I don't believe that."
> "I don't mean his friendship with you. Of course it's deep, he doesn't live with you, and best of all you're a man, you don't have those needs he can't be bothered with. He'd give you a kidney if you needed one."
> "He'd give it to you too."
> "Of course he would. But he wouldn't go to a marriage counselor."

It is with such harsh honesty, as well as with strong, sexually explicit language and a spare prose style, that Dubus avoids sentimentality. As a writer he has developed a distinctive voice: long clear sentences (usually compound), vivid detail for physical objects, accurate description of human emotions and reactions, and understated smoothly flowing sentences at moments of intensity. His language is generally simple and direct, but for accuracy he is willing to use the unusual or formal word: "impuissant," "misogamist," "Faustian." Though he occasionally uses humor and irony, his voice is usually serious, emotionally powerful and simultaneously sympathetic to, but distant from, his characters. His narration is calm, his dialogue good, his words carefully chosen and edited. At his best, writes Joyce Carol Oates, Dubus creates novellas that are "triumphs of voice"—a voice of style that has the quality of "unhurried precision."

Even Dubus's metaphors, though original and effective, have a
certain dispassion to them: "Like a cat with corpses, [my wife]
brings me gifts I don't want"; "His marriage was falling slowly,
like a feather"; "He feels they are not at a hearth but are huddled
at a campfire in a dangerous forest." In one short story, "The
Pitcher," an unfaithful wife effectively uses the metaphor of her
baseball-player husband as she tells him, "All summer I've been
feeling like I was running alongside the players' bus waving at
you. Then he came along."

Dubus often adds breadth and perspective by putting his individuals or families in some larger social, literary or religious
framework. Some characters come out of themselves by meeting
friends at Timmy's Bar; others look to books or plants or records
(classical by day, jazz at night). Dubus's Marines find models of
bravery in Corps legends, especially the heroes of the Chosin
Reservoir. Some characters worry about friends or brothers serving
in Vietnam; others feel concern for the blacks in the South or
the poor on the streets of New York City. Another man in *Voices
from the Moon,* the owner of two ice-cream stores, has an effective
social conscience; he "was good to his workers" and "did not
keep them working so few hours a week that he could pay them
under the minimum wage"; he was even "planning a way for all
workers, above their salaries, to share in the profits, and was
working on a four-day week for his daily and nightly managers,
because he believed they should be with their young families."
(This was a man who had fallen in love with his son's ex-wife.
Dubus's moral universe is never a simple one.)
Dubus also broadens his fiction's scope by literary allusions.
He quotes a passage from St. Thomas More *(The Times Are Never
So Bad),* and at various moments refers to, or echoes such writers
as Conrad *(Lord Jim).* Hopkins, Hemingway, Balzac, Tolstoy,
Shakespeare, Kipling, Faulkner, Zola, Kate Chopin, Rhys, Colette,
de Maupassant, even Joyce, as well as his great literary hero and
teacher, Chekhov. For a writer who is at heart a realist, he makes
surprisingly frequent use of Greek myth: one man, lying with his
love in his arms, "kisses her until she warmly wakes and encircles
him with her squeezing arms; he ascends; he is Prometheus; and
he pauses in his passion to gently kiss her brightened eyes."
Andromache, Oedipus and Icarus make their appearances, and in

celebration of fidelity Dubus uses Aphrodite, the Greek goddess of love and fertility, to comment on contemporary America. Musing about his friend Jack Linhart, who has stayed married despite mutual infidelities, Hank Allison thinks, "Jack is right. He's glad now they stuck it out. He and Terry. He said, I've got a good friend who's also my wife and I've got two good children, and the three of them make the house a good nest, and I sit and look out the window at the parade going by: some of my students are marching and some of my buddies, men and women, and the drum majorette is Aphrodite . . . and she's leading that parade to some bad place. I don't think it's the Styx either. It's . . . some big open field with brown grass and not one tree, and nobody's going to say anything funny there. Nobody'll laugh. All you'll hear is pants and grunts. Maybe Aphrodite will laugh, I don't know. But I don't think she's that mean. . . ."

Far more than to society, literature, or mythology, though, Dubus looks to Catholic belief and practice to broaden the perspectives and expand the framework of his fiction. Sometimes it is an occasional "O Jesus" or "Dear Jesus"; sometimes his characters pray or go to Mass or talk about "Holy Saturday"; sometimes there is a religious allusion in a Dubus title—"Contrition," "Bless Me, Father," "Sorrowful Mysteries." Other characters wonder about God's absence, like the wife who had lost her own faith during college and, thinking about her husband, "did not know whether Lee believed or not. She could not remember ever talking about God to him." There are priests and brothers in his stories, too, most of them good men and wise counselors. Many of Dubus's fictional boys go to Catholic schools (he, himself, attended a Christian Brothers' high school, where he wrote his first stories), and one young boy finds God through guilt: Having almost drowned a young cat, he "looked up into the rain at God." This does not stop the boy, though, from killing the cat the next morning.

As a moralist, Dubus values fidelity, truth, justice and innocence even as he vividly records the failures of marriage and family. His characters sometimes interpret their actions in terms of morality, and one or two of his people go through a process of moral reasoning in the pages of his stories (a dangerous practice for a storyteller, but Dubus keeps it under control). He will even try to redefine a moral term, to make clear that fidelity in marriage involves far more than sexual fidelity. This he does in "The Pitcher," as a wife talks to her baseball-player husband:

> "It wasn't the road trips. It was when you were home: you weren't here. You weren't here, with me."
> "I was here all day. . . . And all those times on the road I never went near a whorehouse."
> "It's not the same."

Dubus also has a strong sense of the sacraments. His characters go to confession or to Mass—folk Masses, parish Masses, quiet weekday Masses. For one character, the Eucharist is a way to avoid loneliness, for another, a way to praise God, for a third, "The Eucharist is the sacrament of love and I needed it very badly those five years" during a bad marriage. And young Richie Stowe himself, in *Voices from the Moon,* wants to become a priest, even as, at book's end, he first experiences the appeal of the hair and arms and hand-touch of young Melissa Donnelly.

More originally, some characters manifest what might be called a "religious imagination," as they use some religious framework or story or phrase to interpret their own experiences of someone else's situation. One young white man from southern Louisiana reads of a black man, Sonny Broussard, who is to be executed for rape and sees his condemnation and death as parallel with Christ's. In another story a suburban housewife, though she has lost her faith, still "tried to pray. She wanted to fall in love with God. . . . Cleaning the house would be an act of forgiveness and patience under His warm eyes." One fifty-four-year-old father comes to love his daughter more in her weakness than in her strength, and realizes that here he resembles God, who loves us humans in our very weakness. And young Richie Stowe from *Voices,* almost thirteen and a daily Mass-goer, "felt always in God's eye," "knew God saw and loved those who suffered, yet still saw and loved him," and was certain that Christ had been in him when he finally forgave his parents for their divorce: "Everyone had to bear a Cross as Christ did. . . . Two years ago his mother moved out and then they were divorced and he (Richie) carried that one, got himself nailed to it, hung there in pain and the final despair and then released himself, commended his will and spirit to God, and something in him died—he did not know what—but afterward, like Christ on Easter, he rose again, could love his days again, and the people in them, and he forgave his parents, and himself too for having despaired of them."

These perspectives expand the world of Dubus's fiction and, together with his spare style, help to control the intensity of emotion and sentiment in his work. But, I should make clear, Dubus is not primarily a novelist of society or literary allusion or religion. His focus is always on his wounded people, with their complex lives and motives, their infidelities and violence and adulteries and "demons," and their unspoken hopes for forgiveness and goodness. Like Virgil, Dubus knows the *lachrymae rerum*— the tears evoked by human experience—and he unfailingly treats his characters with immense and deep compassion.

One more thing should be said: Andre Dubus is a careful artist and craftsman. He loves to write prose; he writes every day on a regular schedule, and lets his story "gestate for a long, long time." He never does an outline and "usually begins with a 'what if.' An idea just comes to me." At that point he needs to know many details about his characters: "I make note of things that may never get into the story. I want to know if they believe in God; if so, do they belong to an organized religion? Ever since the Surgeon General's report on smoking I've thought it was important to know whether or not a character smoked, because it said something about a character. . . . I make notes on the age, the family. The hardest part is to get the characters' employment. I have to find them a job, and then I have to find out something about the job." And when he is ready to write, he writes with great care. Once happy to produce a thousand words a day, he is now content with a hundred. Interestingly, he tapes all of his prose before completing it, testing his word-choice and sentence-rhythms by hearing as well as by seeing. Only then is he prepared to publish.

In 1986, the year of his fiftieth birthday, Andre Dubus has become one of the finest American storytellers. At best in the novella-form, he has done two superb books in *We Don't Live Here Anymore* and *Voices from the Moon.* Caring little for money or fame, he has made himself a master craftsman and gentle father-figure for his characters. His imagination, in its Catholic dimensions, is unusually complex and interesting. A compassionate chronicler of his times, he deserves even more readers, and in this half-century year he deserves as well a quiet toast both for a speedy recovery and continued success as a fiction writer: "Andre Dubus: *Ad multos annos. Ad multos libros.*"

Chronology

1936 Andre Dubus born 11 August in Lake Charles, Louisiana, Son of Andre Jules and Katherine (Burke) Dubus. Siblings: Kathryn Claire, born 1930; Elizabeth Nell, born 1933.

1944 Dubus family moves from Baton Rouge to Lafayette. Enters Christian Brothers School, Lafayette.

1954 Graduates from Christian Brothers High School.

1958 June, earns B.A. (English and journalism) from McNeese State College, Lake Charles, Louisiana. Marries Patricia Lowe. Commissioned as lieutenant in U.S. Marine Corps. Birth of daughter, Suzanne.

1959 Birth of son, Andre III.

1960 Birth of son, Jeb.

1963 Birth of daughter, Nicole. Death of father, aged fifty-nine. "The Intruder." Resigns commission from U.S. Marine Corps as captain.

1964 January, enters M.F.A. program, University of Iowa, Iowa City.

1965 M.F.A., University of Iowa. Lecturer in English, Nichols State College, Thibodaux, La.

1966 Begins lecturing in modern fiction and creative writing at Bradford College, Bradford, Massachusetts.

1967 *The Lieutenant.*

1969 "The Doctor," "In My Life," "If They Knew Yvonne." Latter selected by Martha Foley for *Best American Short Stories, 1970.*

1970 Divorced from Patricia Lowe. "Separate Flights."

1975 *Separate Flights (A Novella and Seven Stories).* Receives *Boston Globe* Award; Laurence L. Winship Award for best book of New England origin. Well reviewed over the next two years in, among others, *Harper's, Atlantic Monthly,*

Washington Post's Book World, Sewanee Review, and, by Joyce Carol Oates, *Ontario Review.* Marries Tommie Gale Cotter.

1976   "Cadence" selected by Martha Foley for *Best American Short Stories, 1976.* Receives Guggenheim Fellowship. Writes eight monthly columns in *Boston Magazine.*

1977   "Adultery." *Adultery and Other Choices.* Well reviewed in *Saturday Review, Washington Post, New Republic,* and elsewhere.

1978   Receives National Endowment for the Arts grant. Divorced from Tommie Gale Cotter. "The Fat Girl" selected for annual Pushcart anthology.

1979   "The Pitcher" selected by William Abrahams for *Prize Stories: The O. Henry Awards 1980.* Marries Peggy Rambach.

1980   Death of mother, aged seventy-eight. "The Winter Father": accepted by *New Yorker,* withdrawn by author when requests for deletions of "vulgarities" are made; published in *Sewanee Review;* selected by Hortense Calisher for *Best American Short Stories, 1981. Finding a Girl in America (A Novella and Seven Short Stories)* receives mixed reviews.

1982   Birth of daughter, Cadence.

1983   *The Times Are Never So Bad (A Novella and Eight Short Stories).* Well reviewed in *New York Times Book Review* by Joyce Carol Oates, among others. "A Father's Story" selected by John Updike for *Best American Short Stories, 1984.*

1984   *Voices from the Moon* (novel). Well reviewed by John Updike in the *New Yorker,* among others. *We Don't Live Here Anymore, The Novellas of Andre Dubus.* Well reviewed. Retires from Bradford College. *Land Where My Fathers Died.*

1985   National Endowment for the Arts grant. *Voices from the Moon* (pb).

1986   Guggenheim Fellowship. "Rose" selected for annual Pushcart anthology. *The Last Worthless Evening (Three Novellas and Two Short Stories).* Receives favorable reviews. Selected as Editors' Choice by *Time*. *The Lieutenant* (novel) reissued. "The Dark Men" anthologized. "A Father's Story" anthologized. "The Fat Girl" anthologized. Loses leg in highway accident coming to aid of injured motorist.

1987　Special issue of *Delta* devoted to a critical study of his fiction. *The Last Worthless Evening* (pb). "Dressed Like Summer Leaves" selected by Shannon Ravenel for an anthology of southern writing. Receives First Schaeffer/New England PEN Award. Birth of daughter, Madeline Elise Rambach Dubus.

1988　Edits *Into the Silence*. "The Curse."

Bibliography

Primary Sources

Collections of Short Fiction

Adultery and Other Choices. Boston: David R. Godine, 1977 (paperback 1979). Contents: "An Afternoon with the Old Man," "Contrition," "The Bully," "Graduation," "The Fat Girl," "Cadence," "Corporal of Artillery," "The Shooting," "Andromache," and "Adultery."

Finding a Girl in America: A Novella and Seven Short Stories. Boston: David R. Godine, 1980 (paperback 1981). Contents: "Killings," "The Dark Men," "His Lover," "Townies," "The Misogamist," "At St. Croix," "The Pitcher," "Waiting," "Delivering," "The Winter Father," and "Finding a Girl in America."

The Last Worthless Evening: Four Novellas and Two Stories. Boston: David R. Godine, 1986 (paperback, New York: Crown, 1987). Contents: "Deaths at Sea," "After the Game," "Dressed Like Summer Leaves," "Land Where My Fathers Died," "Molly," and "Rose."

Separate Flights. Boston: David R. Godine, 1975 (paperback 1976). Contents: "We Don't Live Here Anymore," "Over the Hill," "The Doctor," "In My Life," "If They Knew Yvonne," "Going Under," "Miranda over the Valley," and "Separate Flights."

The Times Are Never So Bad: A Novella and Eight Short Stories. Boston: David R. Godine, 1983. Contents: "The Pretty Girl," "Bless Me, Father," "Goodbye," "Leslie in California," "The New Boy," "The Captain," "Sorrowful Mysteries," "Anna," and "A Father's Story."

We Don't Live Here Anymore: The Novellas of Andre Dubus. New York: Crown Publishers, 1984. Contents: "The Pretty Girl," "We Don't Live Here Anymore," "Adultery," and "Finding a Girl in America."

Novella

Land Where My Fathers Died. Winston-Salem, N.C.: Palaemon Press, 1985 (limited edition).

Novels

The Lieutenant. New York: Dial Press, 1967 (out of print); Cambridge, Mass.: Green Street Press, 1986.

Voices from the Moon. Boston: David R. Godine, 1984 (paperback, Godine: 1984; New York: Crown, 1985).

Edited Work
Into the Silence (stories). Cambridge, Mass.: Green Street Press, 1988.

Short Fiction in Periodicals and Anthologies
"Adultery." *Sewanee Review* 85, no. 1 (Winter 1977): 46–103.
"An Afternoon with the Old Man." *New Yorker* 48 (2 September 72): 27–30.
"After the Game." *Fiction Network* 1 (Fall 1983): 15–19. Reprinted in *The Graywolf Annual: Short Stories.* Edited by Scott Walker. Port Townsend, Wash.: Graywolf Press, 1985, 15–23.
"Anna." *Playboy* 28, no. 6 (June 1981): 137, 174, 236, 238, 240, 242, 246, 248, 251, 253.
"At St. Croix." *Ploughshares* 5, no. 3 (1979): 59–62. Reprinted in *The Ploughshares Reader: New Fiction for the Eighties.* Edited by DeWitt Henry. Wainscott, N.Y.: Pushcart Press, 1985. Reprinted New York: New American Library, 1986, 232–42.
"The Blackberry Patch." In *Southern Writing in the Sixties: Fiction.* Edited by John William Corrington and Miller Williams. Baton Rouge: Louisiana State University Press, 1966, 108–15. Reprinted in *Stories of the Modern South.* Edited by Benjamin Forkner and Patrick Samway, S.J. New York: Bantam, 1978, 78–83.
"Bless Me, Father." *Carleton Miscellany* 11, no. 3 (Summer 1970): 78–88.
"Blessings." *Yankee,* Fall 1986; *Delta* 24 (February 1987): 1–20.
"The Bully." *Sewanee Review* 83, no. 3 (Summer 1975): 394–405.
"Cadence." *Sewanee Review* 82, no. 3 (Summer 1974): 433–56. Reprinted in *The Best American Short Stories, 1976.* Edited by Martha Foley. Boston: Houghton Mifflin, 1975, 80–99.
"The Captain." *Ploughshares* 8, no. 4 (1982): 219–35.
"Contrition." *North American Review* (University of Northern Iowa) 261 (Winter 1976): 21–26.
"Corporal of Artillery." *Ploughshares* 1, no. 4 (1973): 8–13.
"The Cross Country Runner." *Midwestern University Quarterly* (Wichita, Texas), 1967.
"The Curse." *Playboy,* January 1988, 126, 179–80.
"The Dark Men." *Northwest Review* (University of Oregon at Eugene) 12, no. 3 (1972): 3–13. Reprinted in *Soldiers and Civilians.* Edited by Tom Jenks. New York: Scribner's, 1987.
"Delivering." *Harper's,* October 1978, pp. 78–80, 81–83.
"The Fat Girl." In *The Pushcart Prize, III: Best of the Small Presses.* Edited by Bill Henderson. Wainscott, N.Y.: Pushcart Press, 1978–79, 357–71. Reprinted in *Short Story Masterpieces.* Edited by Raymond Carver and Tom Jenks. New York: Bantam, 1987.
"A Father's Story." *Black Warrior Review* 9, no. 2 (Spring 1983): 7–24. Reprinted in *The Best American Short Stories, 1984.* Edited by John

Bibliography

Updike with Shannon Ravenel. Boston: Houghton Mifflin, 1984, 72–94. Also in the American Audio Prose Library, Series IV. Prose Library, 1015 East Broadway, Suite 284, Columbia, MO 65201, 1984 (with interview), two cassettes. Reprinted in *The Substance of Things Hoped For,* 1986.

"Going Under." *North American Review* (University of Nothern Iowa) 259 (Spring 1974): 52–62.

"Goodbye." *Ploughshares* 2, no. 2 (1974): 61–69.

"If They Knew Yvonne." *North American Review* (University of Northern Iowa) 254, no. 3 (Fall 1969): 18–28. Reprinted in *The Best American Short Stories, 1970.* Edited by Martha Foley and David Burnett. Boston: Houghton Mifflin, 1970, 84–107.

"In My Life." *Northwest Review* (University of Oregon) 11, no. 2 (1971): 20–25.

"The Intruder." *Sewanee Review* 71, no. 2 (April-June 1963): 268–82.

"Killings." *Sewanee Review* 87, no. 2 (Spring 1979): 197–218.

"Land Where My Fathers Died." *Antaeus* 53 (Autumn 1984): 190–223. Reprinted in *The Best Short Fiction for 1985: The Editor's Choice: New American Stories.* Vol. 2. Edited by George Murphy. New York: Bantam, 1986, 66–104.

"Love Is the Sky." *Midwestern University Quarterly* (Wichita Falls, Texas) 2, no. 2 (1966): 18–32.

"Madeline Sheppard." *Midwestern University Quarterly* 2, no. 4 (1967): 1–12.

"The Misogamist." *Penthouse* 8, no. 1 (September 1976): 70–72, 74, 114, 146 (with extensive, unapproved editorial changes).

"Molly." *Crazyhorse* (University of Arkansas at Little Rock) 30 (Spring 1986): 86–139.

"The New Boy." *Harper's,* January 1982, pp. 50–56.

"Over the Hill." *Sage* (University of Wyoming at Laramie) 11, no. 4 (Fall 1967): 255–66. Reprinted in *Stories of the Modern South.* Edited by Benjamin Forkner and Patrick Samway, S.J. New York: Penguin, 1981, 77–89.

"The Pitcher." *North American Review* (University of Northern Iowa) 264, no. 1 (Spring 1979): 18–24. Reprinted in *Prize Stories, 1980: O. Henry Awards.* Edited by William Abrahams. New York: Doubleday, 1980, 373–88.

"Rose." *Ploughshares* 11, no. 2–3 (1985): 11–51. Reprinted in *The Pushcart Prize, XI: Best of the Small Presses.* Edited by Bill Henderson. Wainscott, N.Y.: Pushcart Press, 1986–87, 116–49.

"Separate Flights." *North American Review* (University of Northern Iowa) 255, no. 1 (Spring 1970): 10–26.

"The Shooting." *Carleton Miscellany* 14, no. 1 (Fall-Winter 1973–74): 49–60.

"Sorrowful Mysteries." *Crazyhorse* (University of Arkansas at Little Rock) 25 (Fall 1983): 83–94.

"They Now Live in Texas." *Indiana Review,* 10, no. 1/2 (1987): 3–6.

"Waiting." *Paris Review* 21 (Spring 1979): 114–20.

"The Winter Father." *Sewanee Review* 88, no. 2 (Spring 1980): 151–75. Reprinted in *The Best American Short Stories, 1981.* Edited by Hortense Calisher with Shannon Ravenel. Boston: Houghton Mifflin, 1981, 129–49.

Translations

"Jolie, la fille." Arles, France: Actes-Sud, 1986.

Les voix de la lune. Arles, France: Actes-Sud, 1986.

Nonfiction

"After Twenty Years." *North American Review* 271, no. 4 (December 1986): 60–61.

"At Random: Packing It In." *Boston Mgazine,* January 1978, 163–64.

"Footnotes: Of Robin Hood and Womanhood." *Boston Magazine,* December 1977, 233–36.

"Footnotes: Running for Your Life." *Boston Magazine,* October 1977, 203–4.

"Footnotes: To Make a Long Story Short." *Boston Magazine,* February 1978, 122–24.

"Intensive Care." *Indiana Review* 10, no. 1–2 (Spring 1987): 7–8.

"A Laurel for Richard Hugo." *Black Warrior Review* 9, no. 2 (Spring 1983): 104–5.

"Literature." *America* 1, no. 8 (September 1984): 108–9.

"Manners: The End of a Season." *Boston Magazine,* October 1978, 94–95.

"Paths to Redemption: Walker Percy's *Lancelot.*" *Harper's,* April 1977, 86–88.

"Reading: Fiction and the Facts of Life." *Boston Magazine,* November 1977, 58, 60, 62.

"Two Ghosts." *Mid-American Review* (Bowling Green State University) 5, no. 2 (1985): 27–32.

Secondary Sources

Anon. "Andre Dubus: Storytelling, Part of His Art." *Dialogue* (University of Alabama at Tuscaloosa), 14 October 1985, 3.

Anon. "Finding a Girl in America." *Choice* 18 (December 1980): 526.

Bibliography

Baker, J. N. *"Adultery & Other Choices." Newsweek,* 5 December 1977.

Barkham, John. "Teller of Tales." *John Barkham Reviews: The Last Worthless Evening,* 1986.

Broyard, Anatole. *"Adultery and Other Choices." New York Times Book Review,* 20 November 1977, 14.

Cox, Shelly. *"The Times Are Never So Bad." Library Journal* 108 (July 1983): 1380.

Cryer, Dan. "Andre Dubus: Ironic Stories on Timeless Themes." *Newsday,* 30 November 1986, 20.

Curtin, Edward J. "Stories of Conscience." *Berkshire Eagle, Books,* 31 January 1987.

Dahlin, R. "Interview with Andre Dubus." *Publishers Weekly,* 12 October 1984, 56–57.

Escuret, Annie. "Une nouvelle d'Andre Dubus: 'The Doctor' ou le pont, le flot et l'enfant." *Delta* 24 (February 1987): 109–26.

Feeney, Joseph J. "Poised for Fame: Andre Dubus at Fifty." *America,* 15 November 1986, 296–99.

Gies, Judith. "Little Voices." *Village Voice,* 26 November–2 December 1980, 42.

Gilbert, Harriett. "States of Desire." *New Statesman* 108, no. 2799 (9 November 1984): 32.

Gould, Jean. "Last Worthless Evening." *Saturday Review,* Spring 1987.

Granahan, Tom. *"Adultery and Other Choices." Best Sell* 38, no. 5 (April 1978).

Gray, Paul. "Loners and Losers." *Time,* 10 November 1986, 59.

———. *"The Times Are Never So Bad." Time,* 15 August 1983, 61.

Harris, Michael. "Love's Limitations." *Book World, The Washington Post,* 20 July 1975, 3.

Harris, Roger. "Dubus Excels Working the Middle Ground." *Star Ledger* (Newark, N.J.) *Books,* 14 December 1986.

Hathaway, Dev. "A Conversation with Andre Dubus." *Black Warrior Review* 9, no. 2 (Spring 1983): 86–103.

Holmes, Jon. "With Andre Dubus." *Boston Review* 9, no. 4 (July–August 1984): 7–8.

Hubert, Thomas. "The Louisiana Connection in the Fiction of Andre Dubus." *McNeese Review* (McNeese State College, Lake Charles, La.) 26 (1979–80): 74–81.

Kennedy, Thomas E. "The Existential Christian Vision in the Fiction of Andre Dubus." *Delta* 24 (February 1987): 91–102.

———. "A Fiction of People and Events." *Sewanee Review* 95, no. 2 (Spring 1987): xxxix–xli.

———. "The Progress from Hunger to Love: Three Novellas by Andre

Dubus." *Hollins Critic* (Hollins College, Roanoke, Va.) 24 (February 1987): 1–6.

———. "Raw Oysters, Fried Brain, the Leap of the Heart: An Interview with Andre Dubus." *Delta* 24 (February 1987): 21–77.

Kornbluth, Jesse. "The Outrageous Andre Dubus." *Horizon,* April 1985, unpaginated.

Krieger, Elliot. "Andre Dubus Suffered for His Commitment." *Providence Sunday Journal, Books,* 21 December 1986.

"The Last Worthless Evening." Kirkus, 1 October 1986, 1466.

Lesser, Ellen. "Going the Distance." *Village Voice,* 20 January 1987, 50, 52.

Levine, Judith. *"The Times Are Never So Bad." Village Voice Literary Supplement,* 23 (February 1984): 3–4.

Lyons, Gene. "Eavesdropping on the Quotidian." *Nation,* 26 February 1977, 248–50.

———. *"The Times are Never So Bad." Newsweek,* 18 July 1983, 70.

Masinton, Charles G. "Stories Celebrate Strengths of Ordinary People." *Kansas City Star,* 22 March 1987.

Max, Daniel. "Dubus an Unknown Master." *Chicago Tribune,* 22 January 1987.

Mergendahl, Peter. *"Last Worthless Evening," Books, Rocky Mountain News Sunday Magazine,* 31.

Miller, Alicia Metcalf. "Only One Bright Spot in Dubus Collection."*Cleveland Plain Dealer,* 25 January 1987.

Milton, Edith. *"Adultery and Other Choices." New Republic* 178, no. 5 (4 February 1978): 33–35.

Moynahan, Julian. "Hard Lives." *New York Times Book Review,* 22 June 1980, 12.

Nathan, Robert. "Interview with Andre Dubus." *Bookletter* (Harper's Magazine Company) 3, no. 12 (14 February 1987): 14–15.

Oates, Joyce Carol, "People to Whom Things Happen." *New York Times Book Review,* 26 June 1983, 12, 18.

———. "Separate Flights." *Ontario Review,* Fall–Winter 1976–77.

Olson, Clarence. "Life's Litany of Flaws." *St. Louis Post Dispatch,* 14 December 1986.

Penner, Jonathan. "The Making of a Storyteller." *Book World, The Washington Post,* 18 December 1977, E7.

Posesorski, Sherie. "Exploring Places in the Heart." *Boston Herald,* 23 November 1986, 57–58.

Raynor, Janice. *"Last Worthless Evening." Worcester Sunday Telegraph,* 18 January 1987.

Read, Mimi. "Interview with Andre Dubus." *Sunday Times Picayune, Dixie Roto Magazine* (New Orleans), Summer 1984.

Bibliography

Robison, James C. "1969–1980: Experiment and Tradition." In *The American Short Story 1945–1980: A Critical History*. Edited by Gordon Weaver. Boston: Twayne, 1983, 102.

Samway, Patrick J. "Dubus's *Voices from the Moon:* More Mystery and Manners." *Delta* 24 (February 1987): 78–90.

———. "An Interview with Andre Dubus." *America,* 15 November 1987, 300–301.

———. "An Interview with Andre Dubus." 1985, in ms., 29 pp.

Schildhouse, Amy. "Our Dinners with Andre." *Indiana Review* 10, no. 1/2 (1987): 9–20.

Shreve, Anita. "The American Short Story: An Untold Tale." *Coda,* 1983.

Sigal, Clancy. "A Hero in the Worst of Us." *New York Times Book Review,* 21 December 1986, 12.

Soete, Mary. *"Adultery and Other Choices." Library Journal* 103, no. 191 (15 January 1978).

———. "Finding a Girl in America." *Library Journal* 105, no. 1408 (15 June 1980).

Stonehill, Brian. "Memory, the Lens to Look at Life." *Los Angeles Times Book Review,* 14 August 1983, 5.

Sullivan, Jack. *"Adultery and Other Choices," Saturday Review* 5, no. 8 (21 January 1978): 50.

———. "The Way We Live Now: The Fiction of Andre Dubus." *Washington Post Book World,* 11 January 1987.

Sullivan, Walter J. "Separate Flights." *Sewanee Review* (Summer 1975): 544–46.

Swanson, William. "Everyday Survivors." *Ambassador (TWA's Magazine),* 18, no. 10 (October 1985): 90, 92–94, 98.

Taliaferro, Frances. *"Adultery and Other Choices." Harper's,* January 1978, 87.

Taylor, Robert. *"The Last Worthless Evening." Boston Globe,* 19 November 1986, 75.

Thomas, Phil. "Dubus a Fine Storyteller." *Miami Telegram & News,* 1 March 1987.

Updike, John. "Ungreat Lives." *New Yorker,* 4 February 1985, 94, 97–98.

Vauthier, S. "Au-delà du réalisme: 'Sorrowful Mysteries.'" *Delta* 24 (February 1987): 127–50.

Whittaker, S. "Andre Dubus's 'His Lover' and the Classical Temper." *Delta* 24 (February 1987): 103–8.

Wickenden, Dorothy. *"Finding a Girl in America." New Republic* 183, no. 8 (23 August 1980): 37–38.

Yaffe, James. *"The Last Worthless Evening."* Denver Post, Books, 7 December 1986.

Zeidner, Lisa. "Surviving Life." *New York Times Book Review,* 18 November 1984, 26.

Index

Index

Index

Williams, William Carlos, 81
Wolff, Tobias, 115
Work Habits, 118–19, 158
Wouk, Herman: *The Caine
Mutiny,* 24

Yates, Richard, 32, 95–96, 113,
115, 118; *Eleven Kinds of
Loneliness,* 114
Yount, John, 115

Zeidner, Lisa, 9
Zola, Émile, 155

About the Author

Thomas E. Kennedy's fiction and criticism have appeared in *North American Review, Kenyon Review, Literary Review, Sewanee Review, Writers' Forum, Black Warrior Review, Confrontation,* and numerous other literary journals and anthologies. He did undergraduate work at the City College of New York and the New School for Social Research, received his B.A. (summa cum laude) from Fordham University; his M.F.A. in fiction and criticism from Vermont College of Norwich University; and his Ph.D. in the modern short story from Copenhagen University.

Kennedy's fiction has been nominated for the Pushcart Prize many times, and he was cited as an outstanding writer in that volume in 1987. He has been the recipient of a three-year grant for a novel-in-progress from C.C.N.Y.'s Theodore B. Goodman Fund and was a winner of the 1987 Emerging Writer Invitational Competition sponsored by the National Endowment for the Arts and *Passages North* magazine.

Kennedy teaches creative writing in the Vermont College M.F.A. program as well as in the European Division of the University of Maryland. For the past several years, he has lived and worked in Copenhagen with his wife, Monique (a physician and translator), and their two children, Daniel and Isabel. Kennedy and his wife have collaborated on the translations of poetry and prose by a number of Danish writers and compiled the Nordic literary supplement published in 1987 in the Paris-based *Frank,* for which Kennedy is Danish correspondent.

About the Editor

General editor Gordon Weaver earned his B.A. in English at the University of Wisconsin-Milwaukee in 1961; his M.A. in English at the University of Illinois, where he studied as a Woodrow Wilson Fellow, in 1962; and his Ph.D. in English and creative writing at the University of Denver in 1970. He is the author of several novels, including *Count a Lonely Cadence, Give Him a Stone, Circling Byzantium,* and most recently *The Eight Corners of the World* (Vermont: Chelsea Green Publishing Company, 1988). Many of his numerous short stories are collected in *The Entombed Man of Thule, Such Waltzing Was Not Easy, Getting Serious, Morality Play,* and *A World Quite Round.* Recognition of his fiction includes the St. Lawrence Award for Fiction (1973), a National Endowment for the Arts Fellowship (1974), and the O. Henry First Prize (1979). He edited *The American Short Story, 1945–1980: A Critical History.* He is a professor of English at Oklahoma State University and serves as an adjunct member of the faculty of the Vermont College Master of Fine Arts in Writing Program. Married, and the father of three daughters, he lives in Stillwater, Oklahoma.